Working with
Groups
to Enhance
Relationships

Working with Groups to Enhance Relationships

Marie-Nathalie Beaudoin, Ph.D.

Sue Walden

Whole Person Associates
Duluth, Minnesota

Whole Person Associates, Inc.
210 West Michigan
Duluth MN 55802-1908 218-727-0500
Web site: http://www.wholeperson.com
E-mail: books@wholeperson.com

Working with Groups to Enhance Relationships

Printed in the United States of America
10 9 8 7 6 5 4 3 2 1

Editorial Director: Susan Gustafson
Art Director: Joy Morgan Dey
Manuscript Editor: Kathy DeArmond
Production Coordinator: Paul Hapy

Library of Congress Cataloging in Publication Data
Beaudoin, Marie-Nathalie.
    Working with groups to enhance relationships / Marie-Nathalie Beaudoin, Sue Walden.
    192 p. 23 cm.
    Includes bibliographical references.
    ISBN 1-57025-169-X (pbk.)
    1. Marriage counseling. 2. Marital psychotherapy. 3. Couples—Counseling of. 4. Group psychotherapy. 5. Experiential psycho-therapy. 6. Social group work. I. Walden, Sue. II. Title.
    HQ10.B418 1998
    362.82'86—ddc21   98-25401
                                                                CIP

To my beloved husband, Paul Rousseau, who has always believed in me and in this project, and who has patiently and endlessly supported me in achieving it;

To my incredible improv teachers, Sue Walden, Chris Miller, and Doug Kassel, who have creatively expanded my abilities and enhanced my own development as a person;

To my mentor Jeff Zimmerman, whom I respect and admire profoundly as a person and as a professional and who kindly reviewed the narrative sections of this book.

Marie-Nathalie Beaudoin

To my coauthor, Marie-Nathalie, for her initiation and inspiration, which made this book a reality.

Sue Walden

And thanks to all of our participants who happily let us experiment on them.

Table of Contents

©1998 Whole Person Associates 210 W Michigan Duluth MN 55802 (800) 247-6789

PART 1: AN IMPROVISATIONAL PERSPECTIVE

Communication

Cooperation

©1998 Whole Person Associates 210 W Michigan Duluth MN 55802 (800) 247-6789

PART 2: A NARRATIVE PERSPECTIVE
Unmasking Problems

Individuality and Connectedness

Introduction

Being in a supportive, caring, and satisfying intimate relationship is a goal that most individuals hold. Yet for many, willingness, hopes and dreams, desires and attempts yield more sorrow and loneliness than joy. Conflicts emerge from misunderstandings, incompatible gender socializations, fears, different sociocultural experiences and assumptions. Understanding these differences and discovering the ingredients of moments of happy companionship is key to bringing forth more intimacy.

The exercises in this book invite participants to focus on what works in their relationships, to become aware of how they were socialized to act with men and women, and to notice ways of communicating or interacting that brings out the best in themselves and their partner.

These exercises have allowed many women and men to make significant changes in their lives in a short time because they build on people's own life experiences in a playful and empowering atmosphere inspired by narrative ideas. The goal of these exercises is not to instruct people on "how to" live their lives. We believe that each person is the expert in their own lives and that they are the best judges of what is best for them. For that reason, these exercises are designed to invite people to explore possibilities, to become aware of different ways of being and their effects, and to chose the attitude that best fits their intentions.

The book is divided into several sections. The first three sections were written by Marie-Nathalie Beaudoin and introduce the theoretical background of narrative therapy that informs a significant part of the exercises in the book. This section will provide the reader with a clearer understanding of the philosophy and the thinking behind certain activities. It also pinpoints ideas that are helpful in empowering participants to make preferred choices in their lives.

©1998 Whole Person Associates 210 W Michigan Duluth MN 55802 (800) 247-6789

The section on workshop facilitation was written by Sue Walden who has an extensive amount of experience in facilitating a variety of programs. It covers a broad range of aspects to consider when organizing and facilitating a program.

The exercises in Part 1 of this book are drawn directly from improvisational teachings where the emphasis on creating, communicating effectively, and collaborating with team members is very strong.

The exercises in Part 2 focus on understanding and resolving the struggles inherent to relationships. They involve an experiential version of narrative therapy in action. Gender, culture, and differences in general are explored, made visible, and acknowledged. These exercises invite participants to unmask problems, team up against them, and discover their preferred ways of dealing with conflictual situations.

Type of exercises

The exercises in this book have three main characteristics in common:

1. Empowering

They invite people to notice the effects and implications of certain ways of being and empower participants to make choices that best represent their intentions.

2. Experiential

Experience is the essence of our life. Experience is what we remember, what we learn from, what we talk about, what we organize in our brain, what we look forward too. It's basically being alive.

Experience is well recognized for it's teaching power. We all have noticed how telling someone not to do something or giving advice is completely useless unless the recipient is actively engaged in making meaning out of our statement. Most of what is real and remembered comes out of experience. It is said that overall we remember little of what we hear, half of what we read, and most of what we do or experience. Experiential exercises, if meaningful, can thus be very powerful tools for change.

3. Playful

The value of playfulness is remarkable, yet often not appreciated. Playfulness and pleasure are among the primary goals of human beings. Greek philosophers recognized this many centuries ago with the creation of hedonistic groups. Closer to our experience is the example of children. Children acquire a significant part of their learning from play. They discover different ways of being, their motor abilities, and even their intellectual abilities through play. The most successful educational programs are often the ones that entertain children. As we grow older, we are often required to put these abilities aside, not realizing the loss. Yet even as adults we often remember the material on which a professor made a joke and forget a lot of the rest.

Laughing has often been called therapeutic. Laughing groups have been organized in India and laughing festivals in Canada. Biologically, laughing enhances the production of endorphins, which are our natural antidepressants and analgesics. Laughing can lift our mood for a day, allowing us to encounter the world with a more relaxed and flexible attitude. Learning that occurs in a context of fun is thus more likely to be remembered and found meaningful.

Playfulness is particularly relevant to relationships because feeling good is a basic pillar of any relationship. People often create friendship and intimacy based on the fact that they feel good, are happy, and have fun together. Unfortunately, very often , as the relationship progresses through time, the fun fades away or is forgotten under the weight of responsibilities and busyness. That is usually when problems emerge and people begin to spend more time fighting with each other than sharing pleasant activities. Couples find themselves in vicious circles, focusing only on problems. The more the problems are discussed, the less time there is to reinforce why they are together in the first place: to enjoy life.

Playfulness also offers the advantage of offering safety. Many things can be said in a playful tone of voice that cannot comfortably be said in any other tone. Many behaviors can also be tried and explored in an atmosphere of play.

Where does this book come from?

This book emerged from Marie-Nathalie Beaudoin and Sue Walden's meeting in 1993. Sue was facilitating a team-building retreat for the staff of the medical center of Foothill College. This powerful retreat was based solely on experiential exercises derived from improvisational programs. Curious to explore this avenue, Marie-Nathalie thereafter accepted Sue's invitation to try out her improvisation program in San Francisco and became increasingly impressed with the impact of this process on her own, her husband's, and her classmates' lives. It became clear that improvisation exercises triggered much more than enhanced creativity and spontaneity. Most of the participants in the classes were there not to train as professional actors or improvisors but to develop different and preferred aspects of themselves. Since the program was experiential, it brought forth different stories and aspects of participants' lives, created a space to try out new ways of being, and opportunities to challenge inner critical voices. The process in some ways resembled narrative therapy in which Marie-Nathalie was training at that time with Dr. Jeff Zimmerman, Dr. Victoria Dickerson, and Dr. John Neal at the Mental Research Institute of Palo Alto and which had a powerful and meaningful impact on her life. Both experiences eventually triggered Marie-Nathalie's collaboration with Sue to assist people in developing meaningful connections through experiential exercises.

For more information, you may contact Marie-Nathalie Beaudoin at Bay Area Family Therapy Training Associates, 21760 Stevens Creek Boulevard, Suite 102, Cupertino, CA 95014, phone: 408-738-3343, or visit her web site at http://www.voices.com. If you would like to reach Sue Walden, contact ImprovWorks, 1801 Franklin Street, Suite 404, San Francisco, CA 94109, phone: 415-885-5678, or visit her web site at http://www.ImprovWorks@sanfranmail.com.

Fundamentals

Theoretical framework

The exercises in this book are informed by narrative therapy, an approach pioneered by Michael White and David Epston in the last ten years. It emphasizes people's ability to solve their own difficulties when empowered to do so and are allowed to notice their own resources. Narrative therapy owes its name to the fact that it uses a text analogy. In order to make sense of life, we describe all of our experiences as stories that tie all our experiences together. In other words, every time you witness or participate in an event, you mentally organize and arrange the aspects to which you ascribe meaning and importance into a coherent sequence across time that can be called a story. Because all the details of lived experience can never all be encompassed in our story, there are invariably experiences that remain unnoticed and thus unstoried. As a result, the creation of each individual's narrative undergoes a selective process by which only events that fit with the main or dominant story are noticed and ascribed meaning. For example, if you had a dominant story of yourself as unattractive, you would probably not revise your dominant story of unattractiveness when complimented. Furthermore, after a few months, you will probably remember more a critical comment that fit the dominant story than the compliment. Narrative therapy aims at making this storying and selection process visible and facilitates people's escape from "problem-saturated stories." Narrative therapy thus offers a unique and nontraditional way of thinking and working with problems. It differs radically from most common psychotherapies on five levels:

- externalization

- expertise

- social contexts

- intentionality and role of problems

- diagnostics

Externalization

First, a unique aspect of narrative therapy is that it externalizes problems instead of assuming that the client has a flaw or an internal deficiency that must be uncovered and fixed. Specifically it assumes that problems are like habits that have developed as a result of socialization processes and external demands; they are not part of the person's identity but rather result from the influence of something outside the person. In many ways, narrative therapy uses a metaphor very similar to the medical understanding that you catch a cold and you fight it, you don't become a cold. Your identity and lived experience is much broader than your problem story. Hence, during therapy, problems are often personified and explored in detail with their patterns, their habits, and what strengthens or weakens them . . . It is much more effective to fight something that is outside of you than to hate yourself. Specifically, narrative work invites couples to dig into their own knowledge and work as a team to fight problems instead of each other. This approach encourages couples to distinguish their relationship from the problems they might experience in some interactions. For example, a couple can be invited to team up against the habit of blaming instead of engaging in blaming conversations against each other. They can be invited to notice the effects of blaming and discover their ability to resist its influence.

Expertise

Narrative therapy assumes that people, not therapists, are the experts on their own life. As a result, therapist and client (not patient) cooperate as coauthors in an attempt to evict the problem from the client's life and bring forth a preferred life story. Thus the therapist will not mentally interpret the client's statements but will ask what meaning the client attributes to them. This attitude avoids the pitfall of misinterpretation, fosters a context of respect for the individual, and acknowledges the relativity and subjectivity of giving meaning to lived experience. This attitude also means that the narrative therapist minimizes power imbalances between the client and himself. Clients are invited to ask questions of the therapist and even to ask for justifications for the questions asked by the therapist. This promotes an atmosphere of accountability and respect.

Social contexts

Narrative therapy situates all experiences within a social context. Issues such as socioeconomic status, race, gender, power imbalance, patriarchy, religion, etc. are all thought to play a major role in the person's experience. These issues shape people's narratives in specific ways and often support their experience of restraint. An example of the restraining influence of these structures is how men are socially trained to not cry and to refrain from being too emotional.

Intentionality and role of problems

Narrative therapists always assume that given a choice, people would rather not have a problem and that most people do their best to avoid problems. They never attribute intentionality to people with problems or assume that the problem is needed. For example, some theorists view anorexic women as starving themselves with the unconscious intention of manipulating their families and getting attention. Such a view is in radical opposition to a narrative view in two ways: first, a narrative therapist would acknowledge the pain and powerlessness of anorexic women, who are influenced by the requirements of a patriarchal culture in which a woman's worth is defined by her weight; and second, more value would be ascribed to the woman's conscious experience of the problem.

Diagnostics

For two reasons, narrative therapists typically don't diagnose or give medical labels to their clients. First, narrative therapists believe that people have all the resources and the skills that they need to overcome the problems but have not noticed them. Most people can share times when they were able to escape the problem but they don't really know how they did it. Couples, for example, may have experienced a happy honeymoon and at that time, managed to deal with their differences in a constructive way..

Narrative therapists believe couples can escape their current problems and recapture their earlier happiness. They can do this by reflecting upon and reproducing their preferred ways of interacting.

Second, diagnostic labels are believed to have harmful effects. Unfortunately, many people who are labeled perceive all their experiences through the lens of their label and live a more and more restrained life. As a result they usually consult therapists with what can be called a "problem-saturated story of themselves." For example, individuals with learning disabilities often give up activities and perceive many challenges as unachievable because they feel restrained by a diagnosis of disability. Moreover, they are often treated as handicapped and less able by their family members. In narrative therapy, the therapist will invite the client to broaden his experience of himself by externalizing the disability, recognizing it as an entity that can be challenged and limited. In other words, the disability is just a small aspect of themselves and does not deserve so much meaning or restraining power.

Narrative therapy and improvisation exercises

Narrative therapy offers a process that can be compared to the freedom and empowerment people experience when participating in spontaneity, creativity and improvisation seminars. This is why several of the exercises listed in this book were inspired from improvisation exercises. It is important, however, to avoid equating these two approaches in any way as this oversimplification would be blind to the complexities, politics, richness, and challenge of the work. In particular, narrative work focuses on social restraints and discourses that affect individuals while improvisational perspectives use more conventional views of the self and the culture. Nevertheless, improvisation and narrative therapy offers similarities on seven levels. They both:

1. make visible the different stories or versions of the self

2. focus on possibilities

3. challenge the restraints that confine people into specific experiences

4. are made meaningful and real by the presence of witnesses or an audience

5. require collaboration, equality, and trust in the cocreation of stories

6. thicken stories with "yes and" responses

7. allow for reflective moments during which the individual can derive meaning from the experience and think about new situations

Different stories

Narrative therapy and improvisation create space for individuals to experience themselves differently. In narrative therapy, clients are usually questioned as to their moments of success at fighting problems and their experiences of being the way they would prefer to be. Hence by this process, narrative therapy focuses on bringing forth meaningful aspects of oneself. In improvisation classes, actors learn to bring forth aspects of themselves (such as emotions, beliefs, and attitudes) that they have already lived and learn to give them appropriate importance in the playing of different scenes. They rediscover what children are masters at: trying out different ways of being, figuring out what kind of person they would like to be, and creating different stories.

Possibilities

The process of becoming an improvisor or a spontaneous person requires an experience of possibilities; that is it requires that the actor step out of the box defined by his story of himself, by cultural discourses, and by social norms to embody different people, try different experiences and life stories. It is thus an experience of having some space in which to maneuver. Narrative therapy attempts to produce a similar experience by broadening the range of possibilities people can experience and helping them believe they have choices about the type of person they would like to be. In other words, it helps people recognize the different people they are at different times, encourages them to notice the contextual limitations that restrain them, and empowers them to chose their preferred way of being.

Restraints

Most people's actions and thoughts are determined by the fact that they cannot experience themselves in any other way. Their responses to a situation are defined or circumscribed by what they know, how they make meaning of the situation, and what they perceive as the best that they can do. Considering that there are an infinite number of ways of behaving and feeling, people's choices are unnecessarily narrowed by what can be called "restraints." Restraints usually come from the norms, definitions, and expectations in a specific culture. For example, in western culture, men refrain from physical contact with other men because it can easily be misinterpreted. Based on that perception, they will defend themselves or counterattack. An important role of narrative therapy is to question (often called "deconstruct") expectations, assumptions, perceptions, and restraints that have been taken for granted. This process eventually allows individuals to experience more freedom, space, and possibilities in their ways of being and interacting. Improvisation creates a similar context in which participants are invited to step outside of what is expected and normative in the culture and outside the persons they usually are. The context of playfulness offers a safe arena in which alternative ideas and stories can be examined or experienced without regard for the normative cultural restraints. Moreover, participants are constantly requested to try out new characters and embody different attitudes, which broadens their experience of themselves and allows for new or preferred ways of being to be explored. With time, restraints lose their narrowing power and a preferred, freer, and more creative self can emerge from each participant.

Audience

Another similarity between the process of improvisation and narrative therapy lies with the audience. The reaction of the audience plays a large role in the actor's experience of success or failure. Similarly, people's experience of themselves as worthy or not, likable or not, and so on greatly depends on the messages they have received about the "performance" of their "character." For example, if every time a child has the hiccups, parents become impatient, that experience will take on a negative meaning because of people's response to it. Improvisation classes can be therapeutic in four ways: (1) they can allow people who had negative experiences around being noticed to have a positive and alternative experience of the same situation; (2) they offer a safe environment in which to bring forth and explore preferred ways of being by experimenting with different ways of being; (3) they provide a community of acknowledgment through classmates, people who witness the preferred ways of being and contribute to making the preferred story more real and valid; (4) they can challenge the critical voice (also called the "gaze") that most people have internalized by progressively replacing it with the experience of acceptance from the audience in the classroom.

Collaboration and cocreation

Much as a scene is the result of actors collaborating with each other to create an interesting story, narrative therapy involves the therapist and the client as coauthors rewriting the client's experience in a preferred way. It is a collaboration in which both persons offer ideas, co-construct new meanings out of specific issues, and explore the possibilities that can follow. It is a process during which both partners have to be fully present with each other, be transparent about their personal agendas, and listen attentively to the shared experience avoiding as much as possible the tendency to dominate. In improvisation as well as in narrative work, all stories are possible and can be enacted in a preferred way. The critical work is to see all the possibilities, be aware of the social contexts that may color them, and then choose the one that best suits the individual or the scene.

"Yes and" or thickening the alternative story

Improvisation and narrative work require a "yes and" stance. A "yes and" stance is basically an open attitude that focuses on accepting other's ideas and broadening possibilities. It is in direct opposition to a "yes but" attitude that has the effect of narrowing the range of possibilities by focusing on the restraints, the drawbacks, and the obstacles that may be associated with an idea. This attitude has two important effects. First, it fosters collaboration as it assumes that all ideas come from people's experiences and are fundamentally good. It promotes a safe context in which people are free to express themselves and escape silencing judgment or evaluation. Second, it creates a context of exploration by inviting people to add ideas, elaborate on the past and the future, attribute meaning, make connections, and render the story plot more complex and rich. This attitude can be extremely helpful when escaping a problem. Problems are often experienced as paralyzing and narrowing of the mind; they rob us of our sense of agency and ability to see anything else. Everything becomes colored by or associated to the problem. Being stuck on stage is paralyzing in a similar way as a problem takes all our mental space and prevents us from seeing any possibilities whatsoever. In narrative therapy, a later point of the process is to thicken the preferred story so that it becomes as real and valid as the problem-saturated story. Eventually it becomes much stronger. Thickening the preferred story involves exploring the individual's life in quest of a past, present, and future for qualities, skills, or evidences of resistance to the problem. It makes the preferred story more dense, detailed, complex, and rich in experience and connections. With couples, for example, it involves bringing forth past experiences and memories that are consistent with a preferred story of intimacy. Intimate dating experiences are recalled and their preferred story is projected into the future.

Reflexivity

In narrative therapy, a significant percentage of the "restorying" takes place when clients have the opportunity to be in a reflexive position. That is when they are free from the necessity to respond to an interviewer and can "float in" or focus on their experience. This process can be partially reproduced in a improvisation workshop when the facilitator asks for volunteers to engage in a challenging exercise in front of the group. Individuals can choose whether they are ready to try something new or prefer to watch for the time being and imagine what they would do if they volunteered or to just become familiar with a completely different way of being. Thus, such activity respects the different places where individuals might be and allows them to proceed at their own pace. Specifically it (1) gives them the choice of trying something new if it fits with their experience, (2) gives them the control of the timing at which they are ready to try it and, (3) allows them to reflect on the exercise by watching and listening to others either before or after they choose to participate themselves.

Narrative group therapy

The experiential exercises included in this book are useful not only for workshops but also in the context of group therapy, which offers many unique opportunities to participants.

Why are groups helpful?

Groups allow participants to break free from one of the most hurtful effects of problems: isolation. In our culture, problems (whether associated with relationships or not) tend to exclude people from full participation in the community. Participation in a group dedicated to exploring problems and their effects through discussions and experiential exercises directly challenges this isolation and consequently provides many valuable opportunities.

1. Groups provide support and validation.

Since problems invite people to doubt themselves and their abilities, fighting a problem in isolation can be challenging. In contrast, a group of people can support each other, validate each other's resources and strengths, bring forth forgotten moments of freedom from the problem, develop strategies together as a team, and share ideas. It is not uncommon for a group member to resist a problem or to be strong in honor of the group. The feeling of belonging to a community or a group thus directly empowers individuals to stand up to their problem. This is even true outside of meeting times as the experience of belonging remains within them. When faced with a difficult situation, participants may choose to imagine that their team is with them in their imagination or heart.

Groups also provide a place for people to help each other; as the old saying goes "the best way to help someone is to let that person help you." This is true for two reasons:

a) People can discover a lot of their own resources when they help others. For example, many people will become angrier when they see their loved ones mistreated than when they are themselves. Groups can provide this experience; participants' resources will initially be mobilized for others but will thereafter be available for themselves.

b) Problems make people feel worthless and useless in this world. By supporting others, participants experience themselves as worthy and helpful. Helping others brings forth the fundamental feeling of contributing to life and well-being.

2. Groups provide reflexive opportunities.

Groups offer a wonderful opportunity to understand from an observer's perspective the effect of similar problems on other people. Groups allow participants to take a reflexive position in which they can quietly process and observe the effects of problems on others without being swallowed by them.

When someone's problem story is told, participants become aware that people's descriptions of themselves are only a few stories selected from many others; they are not a truth. For example, when a participant shares how depression makes her feel worthless and lists a series of facts that confirm this, observers witness that this is only a story colored by depression. As the group progresses, each participant increasingly notices how problems bias the way others make sense of their experience. These observations are then compared to their own experiences. This process has the effect of reducing the credibility of problem stories (maybe it's not true that I am completely powerless or that I can't be intimate . . .). As a result, participants become more cautious interpreting their experiences and begin progressively to select preferred perspectives and meanings around their lives.

3. Groups provide a space for uncovering the effects of dominant discourses.

Discourses are sociocultural filters and frames of references that insidiously color individuals' thoughts, emotions, and actions. Examples of these are capitalism, patriarchy, and heterosexual dominance. Discourses often have invisible, yet harmful and restraining effects on people who tend to assume that something is fundamentally wrong with them because they don't meet societal norms. The context of a group allows participants to compare their experiences and notice that their problems are similar and directly connected with these discourses. For example, a group on gay/ lesbian relationships can allow participants to explore the effects of internalized homophobia and heterosexual dominance on intimacy. Participants will inevitably realize that what they thought was wrong with them or their partner was the result of internalized homophobia. In a relationship group with heterosexual participants, the effects of gender role specifications can be explored, allowing participants to realize that their struggles are the result of following the cultural prescriptions on how to be a man (avoid commitment, for example) and how to be a woman (seek commitment, for example). Once again, such a process allows people to realize that there is nothing fundamentally wrong with them and to locate the source of their struggles in sociocultural discourses. In groups where these questions are raised, participants, despite their culture, learn to choose preferred ways of being and to protest as a group by supporting each others' alternative decisions.

4. Groups provide consultants on alternative ways of being.

By witnessing other's success and by being exposed to different experiences in escaping problems, participants are exposed to a variety of possible ways of being. They are honored as consultants when they share their strategies, expertise, and knowledge and they have access to consultants by listening to other experiences, ideas, and perspectives. This process is a unique aspect of group therapy. Since most problems are experienced as shameful, people's struggles as well as their successes are typically hidden. This secrecy not only deprives individuals of valuable support and recognition, it also deprives the community of valuable knowledge, expertise, and inspiration. Participation in groups increases hope and allows participants to prove to each other that it is possible to achieve a problem-free lifestyle.

5. Groups provide a safe place for experimenting.

Once participants know each other and trust the respectful atmosphere of the group, they can explore new, different, or preferred ways of being. That is, they can try different ways of interacting and notice the effects on themselves and on others. Groups can thus provide an alternative culture in which there are more possibilities or more space to take risks without being judged. When this process is satisfying in the group, participants feel more at ease performing their preferred self outside in the community.

6. Groups provide an audience.

An identity or a story exists only when it is seen or heard by others. Participating in a therapy group provides opportunities for stories to be shared, discussed, investigated, and circulated.

When a story of success is told, it has real effects on other members. Discussion of these effects reinforces, thickens, and adds to the

©1998 Whole Person Associates 210 W Michigan Duluth MN 55802 (800) 247-6789

initial story of success. Connecting a successful experience with the lives of others somehow make the events more real and meaningful. It brings more significance to it, it confirms its value and implications, and it allows for an observer's perspective. Specifically, it allows participants to look at their success through the eyes of others in the group. This process is incredibly enriching. Not only does it connects everyone to this success and increase the group's hope ("if she can do it, then I can to") it also allows for a profound exploration of the ingredients of these preferred developments.

How do groups work?

Several elements are important for a group to be helpful.

Participants

It is preferable to keep groups to a manageable size to enhance intimacy and safety. Typically groups range from four to fifteen members. It is important to have either a brief meeting or phone conversation with each participant to clarify their goals and their expectations. Including participants with different degrees of experience in dealing with a problem can create a nice diversity of perspective. However, people who are a danger to themselves or others or who struggle with psychosis should be referred to individual therapy prior to joining the group.

Ground rules

It is always helpful to start the first meeting with a discussion of people's needs to ensure the safety of the group. These rules should be generated through the suggestions of participants rather than imposed by the facilitator. This is important for three reasons:

a) When everyone contributes to the process, the commitment to respect the agreements is much stronger and more genuine. People are more likely to follow through on their own our ideas then on those imposed on them. If the list becomes lengthy, categories can always be created so that the list includes everyone's ideas but is manageable. For example, a participant's request for no homophobic statements can be linked under a rule of respect to another's request for no interruptions or for confidentiality.

b) This process also sets the tone for a general atmosphere of collaboration and respect for everyone's needs.

c) It recognizes participants' expertise in their own lives as opposed to placing the facilitator in the role of expert. This is particularly important in a context in which the goal is to empower participants to believe in their own abilities and knowledge.

Format

Different types of groups follow different formats. It is helpful for participants to know what to expect. Will this be a group for sharing personal information, for participating in experiential exercises or gathering didactic information. In general, the more the group is able to bond on the personal level and share experiences of activities together, the better.

Facilitator's role

It is the responsibility of the facilitator to ensure that discussions yield positive effects on people. The way a question is asked and the way language is used must be carefully considered to insure that it will bring forth participants' agency around experiencing themselves in a preferred way. For example, it is not helpful for survivors of abuse to engage in lengthy and vivid recollections of how powerless they felt at the time of the abuse. This may simply re-traumatize everyone. It is the facilitator's responsibility to redirect the conversation to the fact that despite the imbalance of power, the participants tried many things to escape or survive. What does that say about them?

It is also the facilitator's responsibility to ensure that participants see their problems as resulting from life experiences and restraints as opposed to inner defects. For example, if participants struggle with honesty in relationships, this does not mean that they are fundamentally liars or bad people but rather that she became that way as a result of difficult life experiences. The more people are able to separate the problems from their identity, the more they will be able to see, believe in, and experience different ways of being. When participants are encouraged to view problems in that way, they eventually see more possibilities, believe they have more choices, and ascribe meaning to other parts of their lives.

A group's journey

The first meeting can usually be spent setting the ground rules and creating a context in which everyone gets to know each other. It is helpful to invite participants to share not only aspects of their lives that are affected by their problems but also the parts of their lives about which they are proud and satisfied. This sharing can be done by inviting participants to share aspects of themselves one after the other or by using one of the exercises in this book such as "Actually . . . ."

The following meetings can be used to externalize and understand more fully the problems. It is helpful to invite participants to share how the problem affects their thoughts, their emotions, and their actions. If the facilitator has access to a blackboard, it can be very useful for participants to actually see those effects listed altogether in writing. Such a list allows them to circumscribe the problem and gain a more thorough understanding of it. Exercises such as "Voices," "Problem Interview," and "Anger on Trial" contribute experientially to this goal. Participants can even be invited to notice the problem's visits and absences during the week between meetings.

Once the problem is fully externalized for most participants, the facilitator can start each meeting focusing on times where people felt they had resisted the problem. A group exploration and inquiry focusing on how each success was achieved can be initiated so that participants not only ascribe meaning to this success but also understand the steps and the ingredients involved in creating these successes. Moments of resistance can also be experienced within the group through exercises such as "Teaming Up Against It."

At this point meetings are spent balancing some time on under-standing and ascribing meaning to the successes on one hand while continuing to observe the problem and its effect on the other. With time, as participants increasingly restory their lives in a preferred way, the facilitator will want to spend less and less time on the problem. The history and implications of the preferred develop-ments will become the main focus and the central part of each participant's life. A helpful exercise to further develop participants' awareness of their own resources is "Autobiography of a Talent."

When participants have developed their preferred lifestyles, it is important to encourage them to extend their community of support beyond the group and into their day-to-day life. It can be helpful to discuss this process in the group by inviting them to share who has noticed the changes and how their relationships are being affected. Supportive people in participant' private lives can even be invited to attend the group and discuss the new developments.

Some groups end after a certain number of meetings while others continue for lengthy periods of time. It is often helpful for participants who must leave the group to keep with them a concrete reminder of their preferred self and this community of support by providing either a video of the group, a picture, a letter, or a document marking the experience. Several exercises in this book, such as "Lifting Problem-Cloaks," offer rituals or activities to facilitate transitions.

Workshop facilitation tips

Leading a workshop in which people will participate and interact is very different from presenting a lecture. Participants are more likely to be concerned about what might happen, what they will be asked to do, and whether they will be uncomfortable. For this reason, it is essential to take a close look at a variety of elements that can help people feel secure and confident.

Here are some things to be aware of:

The facility

1. Is the facility located in a safe and easy-to-find location

This can make or break any program, so consider it carefully. There are some things you can change about a facility and things you cannot.

If at all possible, tour a facility before you book it for your program, and tour it at the same time of day or night that your program will be held. Neighborhoods that are safe during the day can be very different at night. Ask yourself the following questions:

- Is it easy to find?

- Is there safe and convenient parking

- Is it accessible by public transportation?

- Is the meeting room easy to find?

- How clear is the facility's signage?

- Will they allow you to post directional signs?

- Is this facility congruent with the program and with your organization?

2. Is the building safe and clean? People will not feel relaxed if a space is dirty or seems dangerous.

- Will the facility staff clean the room prior to your program?

- Is the space itself physically secure and free of breakable or dangerous objects?

- Can you eliminate or reduce distractions? A whole wall of mirrors can be a distraction for some types of experiential programs. Likewise, large windows where people can look in can be inhibiting.

3. Does the room have a pleasant ambiance?

- Is the lighting bright but not glaring? Fluorescent lights can appear to vibrate creating low-level anxiety in sensitive people.

- Is there good ventilation?

- Does the room smell fresh?

- Can windows be opened easily?

- Can the temperature be controlled?

4. Seating arrangements

If your participants will be sitting for more than half an hour at any time during the program, you will want to pay attention to the chairs.

- What kind of chairs are provided by the facility?

- Are they clean?

- Are they comfortable—try them out yourself. You may want to consider renting if they are not suitable for your purposes.

The arrangement of chairs prepares people for the experience. Chairs arranged in rows suggest that a lecture will take place, in a circle or semicircle that there will be participation.

If you start off with a small group activity, set up the chairs ahead of time. Be aware, however, that small circles of chairs may appear friendly to some people but cause anxiety for others.

Designing a workshop

1. Know your audience

It adds significantly to a participant's comfort if they believe they are attending the right program for them. As registrations start coming in, find out who is coming and why?

- What is the age range of the participants? This may effect the level of activity.

- Have they been to any or many experiential programs before?

Note: If you have been invited to bring your program to an existing group, you may want to obtain some information about the group.

- What are the organization's goals? Do they often bring in outside programs? What other programs have they presented? How many have been experiential?

- Why did they ask you to work with the group? What do they want to accomplish?

- What are the different roles within the group? Who's who?

- What is the level of experience in the group?

- How well do the group members know each other?

- Are there any pertinent history or significant concerns?

2. In the beginning . . .

Design the early part of the program to gently invite people to participate and set the stage for increased participation.

- Use your own introduction as a way to set the tone for the program: start creating interaction and connections right away.

- Give participants the big picture of the program in an overview and then explain the parts in terms of skills and concepts (describing the exercises will only activate their imaginations about how hard, embarrassing, or silly it might be).

- Select a low-risk icebreaker, mixer, or introductory process that gets participants out of their chairs and eases them into accepting that participation is the norm. A large part of feeling safe enough to participate is to get connected early on to the other participants, reducing the feeling of being in a group of strangers.

3. The body of the program

Design your program for a skill-promoting, successful, and fun experience.

- Think in terms of starting with what participants know; then move into the unknown, progressing in baby steps.

- After every experience, have the group appreciate and acknowledge themselves and the other participants with a round of applause, a cheer, or a standing ovation. Make appreciation and encouragement a vital, continuous part of the program.

- Leave time for people to analyze and discuss their observations and experiences. This allows them to make personal connections to the material as well as benefit from the experience of others.

- Demonstrations are an effective way to give instructions. This can be done by the facilitator(s) or by small groups of volunteers.

- Think through how you will move from one concept to the next; smooth transitions are key to keeping people relaxed and in the moment with you.

- Be sensitive to the pacing. Learning theory says that after being presented with seven chunks of information, people need to practice them before trying to absorb more. We recommend less than seven and as much practice as time will allow.

- If there is a lot of sitting and talking in a section of the design, build in a brief stretch break.

- Start with low levels of risk and build slowly to higher levels. Remember, risk is relative. What is easy for you may feel highly risky for others. When designing an experiential training, consider the following guidelines:

Low risk activities: 99 percent of people consider these to be easy. Most everyone will experience a high level of comfort and success.

- Lecture

- Filling out a paper

- Question and answer period

- Small discussion groups: dyads, triads

Medium risk activities: 50 percent of people consider these to be easy.

- Voluntary participation in group discussion

- Task-oriented mingling

■ Activity that involves everyone equally, whether seated or standing

■ Activity where participant perceives the possibility of judgment

High risk activities: Only 10 percent of people consider these to be easy.

■ Kinesthetic exercises (involving movement)

■ Talking in front of a group

■ Role playing

■ Operating in the unknown

■ Getting personal (showing vulnerability)

■ Skill practice that involves competition and judgment

■ Making a public commitment

■ Singing

Check in occasionally to determine whether the group's needs and expectations are being met. Plan optional and alternative exercises so you can respond with maximum flexibility to the group.

You, as facilitator

Once the participants have arrived, you, the facilitator, will have the biggest single impact on the level of their involvement in the learning experience. Your attitudes and behaviors will set the tone. The goal is to be a walking, talking, role model of openness: relaxed, confident, capable, approachable, and flexible. Below we will look at the effect of both your nonverbal and verbal messages.

Nonverbal:

1. Attitude

Your attitude powerfully influences your success as a facilitator of participative learning experiences. It is shaped by your confidence in yourself, your passion for your subject, and your belief in the value of every person's contribution to the learning process. If your attitude is in the least judgmental, no matter what careful words you use to cover your feelings, the judgments will leak out in some way.

Unfortunately, a judgmental attitude is not something you can alter by just deciding to ignore or sidestep it or even by practicing effective communication skills. It requires that you examine the beliefs and values that create your attitudes.

Ask yourself some pertinent questions:

- How do you feel when someone offers an opinion that is different from yours?

- Can you be accepting without being in agreement?

- Are you open and curious about how people come to their conclusions and interested in their viewpoints?

- How much control over a situation do you want when you are a leader?

- How tolerant are you of ambiguity?

- Do you believe that going with the flow is a valuable skill?

- Can you hold off on forming an opinion while you gather more information?

- How important is it to get participation from everyone in a session?

- Can you let go of outcomes to focus on the relationship building process?

- Do you view problems that come up, including surprises and last minute changes, as "no problem"?

2. Visual elements

Your appearance

In our culture, early assessments about a person are often made based on their appearance. "Attractive" people are often assumed to be credible, confident, capable, friendly, honest, persuasive, successful, etc. Keeping in mind that physical attractiveness is tied more to cultural norms than to actual physical beauty, we, who are "rather average", can balance this assumption by being fit, well-groomed, and making sure that our clothes are always fresh, clean, and neat.

When making the decision on what to wear, do your homework. Ask the sponsoring organization about the dress code or if you are producing the workshop, be sure to include the dress code in your publicity or in the registration information, then you, as facilitator, dress just a little above that.

Your posture and stance

So much is written and said about body language that people are more attuned to it than ever before. Therefore, although what you are doing unconsciously with your body may be merely a comfortable habit, you still could be perceived as tense, closed, or judgmental. This will have a direct effect on participants: they will become tense, cautious, and inhibited in their participation.

So, how do you stand and walk? Have you seen yourself in action, on video? Do you look erect, yet relaxed?

- Try standing with your weight over both feet equally.

- Experiment by standing with your knees locked and then unlocked (not bent, just flexed). Locked knees create tension in your lower body which increases the tension level of your whole body and mind.

- Shift your weight slightly forward on your feet, creating a feeling (and an appearance) of being fully engaged and ready to go.

- Now take a deep breath, letting your upper body lift and open. You will notice your shoulders moving back and your head lifting taller also.

- As you exhale, relax and drop your shoulders and let your arms fall to your sides. Maintain the open upper body and the sense of height. If you feel stiff, jiggle your shoulders around to loosen up.

This stance may feel strange at first; you may even feel exposed and vulnerable. Think back to when prehistorical humans first stood up. They gained an advantage because they could see both food and danger at a greater distance, so could make more effective plans for survival. The disadvantage was that vital organs were exposed. Our feeling of vulnerability as we experiment with this open stance may be a primitive-level reaction to a subconscious perception of danger (remember: speaking in front of a group is listed as Americans' greatest fear).

- Walk over to one side of the room, letting your arms swing freely and naturally.

- When you stop walking, balance your weight over both feet as described above.

- Try this several times, moving to different places in the room until it begins to feel comfortable for you.

- You may have to practice in a variety of situations before you develop this new habit.

Check this out for yourself. Look around: when you see people clasping their hands in front or back of their bodies, or standing with their arms bent and locked at the elbows, do they look relaxed and confident? Experiment: notice the effect of these behaviors on your balance when you move. Often they will inhibit any movement except side to side weight shifting, which, after a short while, can make you look distractingly like a metronome.

Gestures

Add gestures to your balanced stance and movement practice. As you walk around the room, begin talking, letting your arms and hands gesture naturally.

- When you are not gesturing, let your shoulders relax.

- Drop your arms to your sides again.

- Think of this as your arms' rest position.

Facilitators have built-in permission to be expressive. It's expected. Expressive gestures typically are read as a sign of confidence, interest, and enthusiasm.

- Gestures must be natural, of course, or they become distracting.

- Repetitive gestures may also draw attention to themselves.

The secret to natural, expressive gestures is to be well prepared so you can focus on the communication, in the moment, and be honestly enthusiastic about the subject. We strongly recommend that if you are not sincerely interested in and enthusiastic about the content of your presentation, find someone who is and have them facilitate the group.

Eye contact

Making and maintaining eye contact suggests confidence, connection, interest, and integrity; whereas fleeting contact or lack of eye contact, suggest insecurity, deception, or lack of interest.

- When speaking to a group, use your eyes as you would if you were fully engaged in a conversation with one person. View talking to a group as a series of one-on-one communications. Look at people as you talk to them; connect with each person. Their reactions will cue you as to whether you are clear and on track and whether they are uncomfortable, interested, or confused.

- Eye contact acknowledges the listener; it is an invitation to communicate and participate.

- With this in mind, give more eye contact to the quiet people (monitoring their reactions to be sure that you are not making them uncomfortable) and less eye contact to the talkative people (while being careful not to ignore them).

- Even with a large group, connecting with people individually will make it feel like a small, friendly group.

Facial expressions

If you have great interest in your subject, really want to engage participants, and are enjoying yourself, your facial expressions probably will be warm, lively, expressive, and friendly. If, however, you have a low level of facial animation, you may feel cheerful and energetic but your face may not communicate your emotions. If this is true for you, you may want to add face stretches to your regular workout. Try the "Big Face, Little Face" series of stretches:

■ Make the biggest face you can, stretching your face as if it was on a canvas stretcher.

■ Make the smallest face you can, scrunching your face around your nose. Alternate big and small faces five or six times, picking up speed.

■ Move your whole face off to one side of your head, then to the other side.

■ Drag all the parts of your face down to your chin, then lift them up to your forehead.

■ Make a circle with your face, first one direction, then the other.

■ Repeatedly alternate a big face and a little face.

■ End with the tiniest face possible, inhale, then explode your face open with a big breathy sound.

Do this series regularly, a couple of times a day and pretty soon your face will naturally become more responsive and expressive.

Look in the mirror to check your face and its typical expression.

■ What does your smile look like? Does it communicate what you intend?

■ What does your expression say when your face is at rest? I've seen faces at rest that look angry, stern, bored, and sad, although that's not how the person feels.

- Experiment with putting energy into your face to move it out of neutral so that your outside is more consistent with your inside.

- People with heavy moustaches or moustache-beard combinations usually have to smile more broadly for their smiles to be seen.

Acknowledging behaviors

When you are sincerely interested in other people and their input, you instinctively act in ways that acknowledge your connection with them.

- You nod your head.

- When listening, you tilt your head slightly to one side.

- You maintain eye contact.

- You smile or use other appropriate expressions.

Observe yourself and others and experiment with acknowledging behaviors to see how they encourage participation.

Listening

A challenging part of facilitating participative learning experiences is listening fully when people participate. There can be a strong temptation, during a group discussion, for example, to tune out temporarily and start thinking about what's next on your agenda.

- Every contribution during a discussion can support your learning objectives.

- A participant may use questions as a way to indirectly express concerns.

- In experiential learning, it is often the discussions that make sense of the experience and anchor the learning, so it is imperative that you are fully present and listening.

You can listen with your eyes as well as your ears, observing whether participants are interested, confused, resistant, in tune, enjoying themselves, uncomfortable, etc. This information can guide you to

©1998 Whole Person Associates 210 W Michigan Duluth MN 55802 (800) 247-6789

change your approach, move on, add or drop things from your design, or stop everything and check in.

3. Vocal elements

Volume

Your speaking volume will vary according to the size of the group.

- If the group is large and the experiences will be noisy, you may need to provide amplification.

- Some parts of your vocal range will carry better than others. Get feedback on this from associates.

- Learn to use diaphragmatic breathing. This will help preserve your voice when you are working with a large and noisy group for a day-long session.

- Keep in mind, that a voice that is too loud can be intimidating or sound like you're shouting; a voice that is too soft can make it too easy for people to mentally wander off.

- Increase your volume to raise the energy level.

- Decrease your volume to make what you are saying sound very important, especially when you also slow down.

By listening to yourself and watching the group, you can modulate your volume appropriately and add the variety needed to keep your presentation interesting and people alert and engaged.

Pacing and pauses

Variety and appropriateness are key to effective pacing.

- Find the balance between speaking slowly enough for people to comprehend what you are saying, yet not so slow that you sound bored or condescending.

- Increasing your speed can raise your own and the group's energy level; slowing down can create a sense of focus and importance.

Pauses and silence are useful tools in any communication.

- Pauses allow information to sink in, ideas to germinate, and thoughts to gather.

Consider pacing and pauses when moving from one experience to the next.

- Find the pace that leaves people wanting more.

- Develop processes that will allow even people who respond slowly to participate without boring those who are ready to move on quickly. Example: have everyone write responses/ideas then have everyone share at least one in triads or small groups.

The first discussion question is often followed by silence while people gather their thoughts.

- Take a deep breath and exhale slowly before jumping to the conclusion that the participants have nothing to say or didn't get anything from the experience.

- Observe closely. Participants' facial expressions will tell you whether you need to give them more time, reframe the question, or add a comment or example.

- If these initial silences keep happening, you may wish to ask for a show of hands in response to an initial question.

Pitch

Audiotape yourself during workshops to analyze objectively the way you use your voice.

- Monotone or singsong tones are distracting and can make it easy for participants' minds to wander.

- High pitched, shrill voices can be annoying. To some people, they sound like fingernails scratching a blackboard.

Notice how you end sentences. Do they usually end with a rising pitch, as though you are asking a question?

- If you are not asking a question and you continually end with a raise in pitch, it can sound like you are seeking approval.

- Used selectively, raising your pitch at the end of a sentence can invite input and involvement.

Ideally, because your attention is focused on what you are saying, how much you enjoy sharing it, and the people to whom you are speaking, your voice has an appropriate and varied level of animation, including volume and pitch.

Verbal elements

1. Quantity of information

Say what you have to say simply, clearly, and directly.

- Limit amount of detail so participants can make their own discoveries.

- Too much explanation implies there's a right and wrong way to carry out an exercise and, worst of all, implies that you're trying to save participants from any possibility of making mistakes (mistakes need to be an okay part of the discovery process in an experiential learning setting).

- Initially, limit the number of learning objectives to two per activity, any more and participants may get lost.

- As mastery increases, add to the challenge by offering more learning objectives if this is appropriate.

- Give participants just enough information about the learning objectives to focus their attention during the process but still allow them to explore and discover.

2. Choice of words

- Stay focused.

- Be aware of the effects and implications of the words you choose; for example, when talking about significant others, be careful not to use only heterosexual language which will marginalize or alienate gay or lesbian participants.

- Watch out for unrelated digressions and keep related digressions brief.

- If you believe that your explanation wasn't clear the first time, rather than explain again, suggest: "Let's walk through it once," or "Let's try it!" This helps participants get out of their heads and into their bodies, focusing on doing it now rather than figuring it out first.

Encouraging, acknowledging words

Look for ways to acknowledge, encourage, and appreciate contributions with words that do not evaluate or judge:

- Say "thank you" with a smile.

- Connect the contribution to the learning objective.

- Ask the group to give themselves or each individual a hand.

Judgmental words

When presenting a structure, objective, goal, etc., use neutral adjectives to describe the desired outcome. Avoid evaluative or judgmental terms that convey that there is a better, best, good, poor or wrong way to do something.

In an effort to be encouraging and supportive, you may hear yourself using the word "good" or even "great" to describe someone's contribution. This sounds helpful, but often isn't.

- "Good" is:

  Nonspecific

  Not particularly helpful

  Gives no information about what worked, so the learning can be repeated

- The effect of "Good":

  Implies something else is bad

Suggests that others should be careful to do as well

Encourages and creates approval seeking

Encourages inside-the-box thinking

Discourages risk

Gives the facilitator all the power

Invites evaluation and comparison

- "Good" can imply:

I agree

I approve

You think like me; we're in the same camp, on the same side

You have worth

That's a creative answer

You are a good person

That is the right answer

You understand the concept; you got it right

There is one interpretation

You are smart

You matched my standards

It's much more helpful to explain what worked (teach them how to fish) rather than shortcut with a label like "good" (handing them a fish).

Conclusion

As you can see, creating an environment that encourages participation and risk-taking is a many-layered challenge. A lack of attention to any of the elements addressed here can sink even your best intentions.

So we recommend that you plan thoroughly and in great detail ahead of time; then when it's time to deliver, let go of any attachment to those plans and be your most attentive, responsive, charismatic self.

Part 1

An Improvisational
Perspective

Communication

Anyone Else?"

In this active game, participants get acquainted in a playful way by sharing their values, hobbies, and preferred aspects of relationships.

Goals

To get acquainted with fellow participants.

To identify preferred ingredients of relationships.

To share aspects of oneself that are meaningful.

Group size

8–16 participants.

Time

20–30 minutes.

Materials

Chairs (one less than the number of people)

Process

1. Welcome participants, then ask them to move their chairs into a large, evenly spaced circle. Do not bring a chair for yourself.

2. Introduce the exercise by providing the following information:

   - In this game, the goal is to reveal something invisible about yourself: your values, hobbies, activities, relationships—and see who else in the group shares this aspect of your life with you.

   - It can be as simple as your favorite activity or type of food or an experience you like to share with an intimate partner.

   - Do not reveal something that makes you feel uncomfortable.

   - Make sure to take care of yourself and each other so nobody gets hurt.

- When it's your turn, make your statement, then ask "Anybody else?" Others who share that aspect of your life must stand and quickly move to another chair trying to playfully avoid being caught in the middle without a chair.

3. Stand in the middle of the circle and make a statement such as, "I like to give massages to my partner," then ask "Anybody else?"

4. As the people who share that statement get up out of their chairs and move to another empty chair, you should quickly find a chair and sit down.

5. This will mean that someone will end up without a chair.

6. The person who remains standing moves to the middle of the circle and shares a statement, then asks, "Anybody else?" and so on.

7. Conclude the game by asking the participants some of the following questions:

   - How did it feel to share these aspects of yourself?
   - Did you discover some commonalties with other participants?
   - Did you worry about what you would say?
   - Why is it important in relationships to recall and talk about moments that we enjoyed?
   - What effect does it have on each partner to know more about the other's preferred interactions?

©1998 Whole Person Associates 210 W Michigan Duluth MN 55802 (800) 247-6789

Post-it Puzzle

This activity offers a powerful way to experientially discover each person's strategies to communicate in an effective and efficient way.

Goals

To invite participants to notice their ideas and strategies on how to send clear messages.

To increase participants awareness of the effect of their way of communicating.

Group size

Unlimited number of pairs.

Time

30–45 minutes.

Materials

Puzzle Solution 1 and **2** worksheets; cardboard; ten 1-1/2 x 2 inch Post-it notes for each pair (Post-it notes can be cut into equilateral triangles in advance as shown).

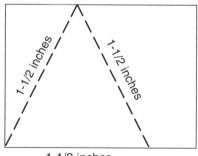

1-1/2 inches

Process

1. Invite participants to sit back to back with their partner along a

straight line. Allow three feet between them and the pairs on either side of them.

2. Introduce the activity by telling the participants:

   ■ This game involves communicating a set of instructions in a limited amount of time.

   ■ You must use only verbal communication to complete the task. Don't look over your shoulder.

3. Distribute the **Puzzle Solution 1** to all the partners facing in one direction and the cardboard and ten Post-it notes to their partners sitting behind them.

4. Provide the following instructions:

   ■ Partners with **Puzzle Solution 1**, you will clearly communicate with your partners the arrangement of triangles you see on your worksheet.

   ■ Partners with Post-it notes, you will arrange the triangles on your cardboard, according to your partner's instructions. You may ask questions.

   ■ You will have 5 minutes to complete the task. Begin now.

5. After calling time, allow a few minutes for partners to compare the worksheet to the **Puzzle Solution 1** and discuss their process.

6. Ask partners to change roles; distribute the **Puzzle Solution 2**, cardboard, and Post-it notes, then repeat the process.

7. Conclude the exercise by asking participants to discuss some of the following questions:

   ■ What worked and what didn't work in achieving this task?

   ■ What strategies did you discover to facilitate the process?

   ■ What caused miscommunication?

   ■ Did certain words have different meanings for each of you? Can you share examples?

   ■ How is this exercise similar to or different from your day-to-day communications?

PUZZLE SOLUTION 1

PUZZLE SOLUTION 2

Twins

This game invites participants to collaborate with and be extremely attentive to their partner (twin) in a playful way. It requires cooperation, concentration, and complicity.

Goals

To be focused and fully present with a partner.

To cooperate and practice not leading and not being led.

To listen very carefully.

Group size

2–20 participants.

Time

30 minutes.

Materials

None.

Process

1. Instruct participants to form trios and sit together in small circles.

2. When everyone is in a group, give the following instructions:
   - Two people in your group will be identical twins; this means that they will share everything they do including answering questions exactly at the same time and in the same manner.
   - The third person in your group will interview the twins about simple day-to-day issues such as their favorite type of ice cream or where they went on their last trip. The twins, while looking at each other carefully, will *slowly* give the exact same answer at exactly the same time!

■ After answering ten questions, change roles and form a new pair of twins so that each member of your group will have the opportunity to play with each role.

☞ *Facilitator can also call "Switch."*

3. After giving participants 15 minutes to experience these roles, reconvene the group in a large circle. You may invite one pair of twins who feel that they have a particularly intense connection to perform in front of the whole class.

4. Invite participants to discuss this exercise by asking the following questions:

■ How was the experience of being twins?

■ Did you develop any strategies to be fully connected?

■ Was there any leader in the twins or did both partners share equal responsibility for the answers?

■ How were you able to pace your timing?

■ What abilities did you notice you had that helped you succeed in this exercise?

■ How would it be in a couple's relationship to always listen that way?

Word Flip

In this active game, participants brainstorm alternative words for personal characteristics usually described in negative terms. The flip of the word "lazy" could be "knows how to relax."

Goals

To discover alternative interpretation for behaviors often perceived negatively.

To consider different perspectives.

To practice silencing a critical voice.

Group size

6–20 participants.

Time

30–60 minutes.

Materials

Easel paper; markers; masking tape; bell or whistle (optional).

Process

1. Introduce the exercise, presenting the following information and offering your own examples:

   ■ Words are powerful. What we say influences our thoughts, our emotions, and our actions.

   ■ It makes a difference whether I call you compulsive or committed, lazy or relaxed. It makes a difference in how I think about you and in how you respond to me.

   ■ By choosing respectful rather than negative words to describe a person, we can actually change our attitude toward that person—and their attitude toward us.

- At first, we have to concentrate on selecting and using respectful words, but the rewards that follow will soon make the process easy and natural.

- In today's activity, you'll have a chance to practice this shift in perspective.

2. Form two teams of equal size. Ask the teams to move to separate areas of the room, then give each team several sheets of easel paper, masking tape, and a marker and ask them to tape the easel papers on the wall.

3. Give the following instructions:

- Form a line facing the easel paper taped on the wall.

- Select one person to act as a recorder and give that person the marker.

- When the game begins, I will call out a negative characteristic. You will have 1 minute to brainstorm as many neutral or alternative words as possible and to write them on your easel paper.

4. Call out the first word on your list. Select words from the list that follows (alternative perspectives follow each negative word) or develop your own list.

boring	peaceful, quiet, thoughtful, tranquil, relaxed
show-off	energetic, creative, good actor, fun, playful, dynamic
lazy	knows how to relax, tired, depressed, preoccupied
hysterical	emotional, excited, fun, energetic, active, vigorous
crazy	unique, original, creative, different, artistic
stupid	slow, thoughtful, mistaken, tired, uninformed
slow	thoughtful, cautious, careful, patient, meticulous
selfish	assertive, has self-respect, balanced

dependent	caring, loving, intimate, empathic, altruistic, compassionate
jealous	caring, loving, intimate, committed, invested, attached
snobbish	shy, elegant, self-conscious

5. After 1 minute, ring the bell, blow the whistle, or call time in some other way.

   Ask each team to count their words or phrases and then share them with the entire group.

   Announce the first-round winner (the team with the most words), then give the following instructions:

   ■ Reform your lines, maintaining the original order.

   ■ The person on the left end of the losing team's line should now join the winning team, moving to the right end of that team's line.

6. Repeat steps 4 and 5 until you have called off all the words on your list. At the end of the game, the team with the most members is declared the winner.

☞ *If everyone in the group moves to one team before all the words are used, form new teams and continue.*

7. Conclude the activity by asking participants to discuss the following questions:

   ■ How hard was it to consider alternative perspectives?

   ■ Why is it that with lots of words available, it's the negative ones that come spontaneously to our minds and our mouths?

   ■ Imagine yourself stopping the critical voice within you. How would you feel about yourself? How would your relationships be affected?

8. Send participants away with a challenge:

   ■ During the next week, explore the benefits of considering other perspectives.

- Every time you stop the critical voice, it loses power over you.
- By the end of the week, you'll find that considering alternative meanings for people's attitudes and behaviors has positive effects on your relationships.
- Remember that people always have a reason to do what they do.

Sound/Action Ping Pong

In this exercise, participants focus on being open, receptive, and validating; they are invited to concentrate on what others have to offer and to listen before answering.

Goals

To practice validation and listening to other's experiences.

To notice one's preferred ways of being listened to.

Group size

6–10 participants.

Time

30 minutes.

Materials

None.

Process

1. Ask participants to form a circle large enough so everyone has approximately two feet of space around them in which to move.

2. Give the following instructions:

   - In this game we will experience different ways of listening and receiving information.

   - In the first part of the exercise, you will make a physical and verbal statement about an emotion to someone in the circle. The statement and gesture can be very simple (waving your hand and saying "I'm so sad to leave") or more complex (shouting "I'm so happy," jumping in the air and turning).

   - When you receive a statement, don't acknowledge it in any

way, merely watch, then create a statement of your own and send it to someone else in the circle. I'll begin.

3. Once every participant had a chance to receive a gesture, move to part 2 of the exercise where participants acknowledge the action that is sent to them. Instruct them to play with different ways of acknowledging what they receive until they find a way that fits for them.

   ■ We'll now repeat the activity, but this time respond to the senders by replicating their statements, facial expressions, and body movements. For example, if the sender looks sad and says, "I feel sad," you might respond with an equally sad expression and the words "I understand that you feel sad." Then after acknowledging what was received, you send something completely different to someone in the group. For example, "I hate olives."

   ■ There are many ways to validate people's emotions.

4. When everyone has received and sent statements at least one time, ask participants how they experienced this exercise.

5. After hearing their feedback, the following questions may expand the discussion:

   ■ How did you enjoy the exercise?

   ■ How did it feel to not be acknowledged when you initially sent statements?

   ■ What kind of acknowledgments did you prefer?

   ■ What were different ways of acknowledging?

   ■ How did it feel to know that you were heard?

   ■ How would acknowledging affect conflict management?

   ■ Why is it so important to acknowledge?

   ■ What do you want to remember from this exercise?

Switch Story

This activity requires that participants bring their attention into the present moment and thus gives them a rich experience of listening and cocreating with others.

Goals

To practice being present.

To practice listening carefully.

Group size

Unlimited numbers in groups of 2 or 3 participants.

Time

20–30 minutes.

Materials

None.

Process

1. Invite participants to form groups of two or three people and to sit close together on chairs or the floor, separate from other groups.

2. Introduce the exercise with the following information:

   ■ The members of your group will collaborate to create a story. One person will begin. When I say "Switch!" stop in midsentence. Your partner or the person to your right in the group will continue the story from where you left off.

   ■ In order to maintain the continuity of the story, partners will have to listen carefully enough to be ready to finish the word or the sentence of their coauthor.

   ■ This process of creativity becomes like a dance in which partner's stories merges, as if they were one author.

- Your only goal is to collaborate with your partner(s). The laws of realism, plausibility, budget, or physics may be ignored.

3. Ask the group for story ideas, then combine several to suggest a creative story title that all the small groups will use. For example, a mode of transportation rarely used in this country and a planet will create a title like: "The Rick Shaw Riders of Pluto."

4. Ask a volunteer from each group to start improvising a story based on the title.

5. After about 15 seconds, call out "Switch!"

6. Pick up speed in the switching as time progresses.

7. After 15 minutes, conclude the exercise by asking the participants to discuss some of the following questions:

   - How did you experience the exercise?

   - Were you surprised by the intensity of your listening?

   - What strategies did you develop to make sure that you could stay in the present time and be ready to complete each other's words and/or sentences?

   - How was the process of coauthoring a story?

   - How was the experience of being completely open to your partner's choices in the story telling?

   - How could this experience apply to your relationships?

Create a Shape

This activity invites participants to cooperate and communicate what they are doing as they create different shapes with their eyes closed.

Goals

To clearly communicate with words only where you are relative to others.

To cooperatively accomplish a task, sharing leadership.

To stay open to others' ideas.

Group size

Unlimited; in groups of 6–10 participants.

Time

15–25 minutes.

Materials

None.

Process

1. Invite participants to make standing circles of 6–10 people each, holding hands with their neighbors.

2. Introduce the activity with the following instructions:

   - Imagine that your circle is a flexible rope. You can use that rope to create shapes: shapes with curves, shapes with corners.

   - In this activity, I'll ask you to create those shapes with your eyes closed.

   - You can do this effectively by verbally communicating with each other your relative positions. Speak clearly, listen carefully, and tune into the collective experience.

- Now close your eyes and by communicating verbally with each other, form your group into a circle. When your group agrees that the circle has been created, you may open your eyes and check.

3. Continue the process by asking participants to close their eyes and form another, more complex shape: rectangle, equilateral triangle, pentagon, isosceles triangle, etc. Repeat several times.

4. Have the groups close their eyes again and assign them another shape: a square; and so on with more complex shapes.

5. Conclude the activity by asking the participants to discuss the following questions:

- What strategies did you develop to effectively communicate with each other?

- What interfered with achieving the group's goals?

- What did you notice yourself focusing on?

- Was it hard to share the leadership position?

- Were some of you silent or silenced in the process?

- What did you learn about yourself during this experience?

- How can the experience of this exercise be relevant in your relationships?

Bouncing Story

In this story-telling game, participants build a cohesive story by completing each other's sentences.

Goals

To listen closely and sustain eye contact with a partner.

To cocreate a story through cooperation and flexibility.

To let go of preconceived ideas.

Group size

Unlimited; in groups of 5–12 participants.

Time

15–30 minutes.

Materials

None.

Process

1. Invite the group to form standing or seated circles of 5–12 people.

2. Introduce the exercise, presenting some of the following information in your own words:

   ■ Listening to others is a challenge because before they finish speaking, we start evaluating what they are saying, or start thinking ahead to what we will say when our turn comes.

   ■ People often have very different styles or approaches for activities such as creating a story. In this exercise you can try doing it someone else's way and practice with their style.

- Individuals struggling with shyness and lack of entitlement will be challenged by maintaining eye contact with their partners.

- Imagine that this story is being audiotaped and will be sold as a book on tape. Keep in mind we want to make cohesive story.

3. Provide a title for the story that will be used by all the groups. Hint: A title can be created by asking the group to name a common item: piece of furniture, appliance, utensil, tool, etc., then add the word "magic" (i.e. The Magic Spatula).

4. Continue with the following instructions:
   - The starting player in each circle should look into the eyes of another player and begin the first sentence of the story.
   - When halfway through the sentence, the first player stops. The player being looked at must complete the sentence while maintaining the eye contact with the starting player. It is critical that the sentence is completed in a way consistent with what the first player initiated, even if that sentence is not your style. It is part of the game to finish that sentence in the most grammatically correct way. You may even be invited to complete a word.
   - Once the sentence is complete, the second player then chooses another player to make eye contact with and begins the second sentence.
   - Continue passing the story, a half-sentence at a time until I call time.

5. Conclude the game by asking the participants to discuss some of the following questions:
   - What did each of you find the most challenging in this exercise?
   - What did it require you to do?
   - What would you like to remember about how you dealt with the situation?

- Did you listen in a way that was different than usual?
- What got in the way of listening?
- Does this exercise remind you of any relationship process?
- When are the skills involved in this game the most helpful in a relationship?

Variation

Story Toss: This variation forces everyone to listen carefully the entire time since they are given no notice of when their turn is coming.

1. Form groups of 5–7 participants and give each group a Nerf ball.

2. One person in each group starts the story. When the facilitator yells "Toss!," the storyteller tosses the Nerf ball to another person in the group who must complete the sentence and move the story forward.

3. This player continues the story until the facilitator yells "Toss!" again, then tosses the Nerf ball to someone else in the group.

4. This process continues until the facilitator signals a conclusion.

Emotion Mirror

This exercise allows participants to notice their own nonverbal emotional expressions and explore another person's way of expressing various emotions.

Goals

To explore a wide range of ways to express emotions through facial expressions and body language.

To notice different ways to express them.

Group size

Unlimited pairs.

Time

20 minutes.

Materials

Emotions handout.

Process

1. Invite participants to pairs up with someone of similar height and stand about two feet apart, spreading out around the room.

2. Introduce the exercise with the following information, perhaps offering some of your own examples.

   ■ Many people are uncomfortable with emotions. But emotions provide us with important messages. A message may be that something is happening, something is threatening, or something is right.

   ■ It is helpful to acknowledge our own emotions, be able to recognize them in our body and in the bodies of people around us, especially those who are significant to us.

3. Distribute the **Emotions** handout to stimulate ideas for participants to use, then provide the following instructions:

   ■ Identify one of your pair as A and the other as B.

   ■ Partner A, you will begin by slowly expressing an emotion with either your facial expression, body movement, or a combination of the two. Continue by slowly changing from one emotion to another, including all the in between steps that are required to go from neutrality to for example, joy to excitement and then slowly to fear or whatever you might choose.

☞ *You may want to demonstrate with a partner while explaining.*

   ■ Partner B, face A, and mirror the exact expression and body position of your emotion-leader at the same time.

   ■ After 30 seconds, I will call out, "Change the lead." Partner B, you will then take over the lead beginning with your current expression and body position and moving slowly into emotions of your choice.

4. Change the leadership after 30 seconds for several more turns, then progressively decrease the time until the turns are 10 seconds each.

☞ *It is interesting to end this exercise by instructing participants to share the leadership and follow each other.*

5. Bring the exercise to a gentle end by asking the participants to slowly come back to a state of neutrality, then give themselves a hand.

☞ *Note: this game is challenging and arouses tension about which emotion to choose, so keeping the time each partner leads short is a good idea. In addition, this game may also raise the voice of self-criticism similar to when we see ourselves in a real mirror.*

6. Conclude the activity by asking participants to discuss some of the following questions:

   ■ What emotions were aroused simply by doing this exercise?

- How was the experience of mirroring someone else's emotions?

- Did expressions of fear or discomfort affect you?

- Was it harder to lead or to follow your partner?

- What were the implications of each role?

- Were you surprised by the variety of facial expressions that can be displayed?

- Had you ever noticed the subtle movements that lead to a facial expression before?

- How was it to determine which emotion your partner was displaying?

- Can you think of any gender differences either in the expression of these emotions or in the noticing of them?

- How would it be in a relationship if you were to pay such close attention to your partner's emotional reactions during a conversation (without mirroring)?

- Why might the information conveyed by nonverbal cues be important to notice in intimate relationships?

EMOTIONS

aggressive	puzzled
bored	sorry
disappointed	withdrawn
excited	cautious
helpless	exhausted
interested	jealous
negative	optimistic
regretful	relieved
stubborn	shy
annoyed	proud
confused	guilty
embarrassed	envious
frightened	enthusiastic
humiliated	peaceful
loved	loved
paranoid	mischievous
satisfied	frustrated
suspicious	curious
bashful	sure
determined	relieved
ecstatic	apathetic
happy	anxious
innocent	angry
miserable	discouraged

Uncovering Invisible Rules

This activity helps us recognize how the stories and ideas we have about a situation create expectations, rules, and assumptions.

Goals

To notice the effect of ideas and stories on our behavior.

To become aware of our experience when expectations, stories, and rules aren't followed as we had assumed they would be.

Group size

Any number of pairs, space allowing.

Time

20–30 minutes.

Materials

None.

Process

1. Lead participants directly into the game, just mentioning that it is an exercise about observation and assumptions. Invite the participants to stand facing a partner with about five feet between them, arms relaxed at their sides. Provide the following instructions:

   ■ You have 15 seconds to observe your partner closely. Begin now. (allow 15 seconds)

   ■ Now turn around so you cannot see your partner and change three things about your physical appearance. When you are done, raise your hand.

   ☞ *Note: you may want to play music during this period, so that they can't hear any of the changes being made.*

2. When all hands are up, continue with the following instructions:

   ■ Turn around. Look carefully at your partner, noticing any changes. Then take turns telling your partner what you saw.

   ■ When both partners are finished, point out any changes your partner missed.

3. Ask participants to change partners; then repeat the instructions in Step 1, this time instructing them to change five things about their appearance.

4. Repeat Step 2.

☞ *If you are coleading the workshop, have the coleader take over for the final part of the exercise.*

5. Repeat Step 3 again, but this time, after the partners turn their backs to each other, ask them to state what color their partner's eyes are.

☞ *Note: People will invariably protest at this final instruction because they expected and assumed a different set of directions and operated accordingly.*

6. Conclude the activity by asking participants to discuss some of the following questions:

   ■ What did you expect when you first heard the instruction: "You have 15 seconds to look at your partner and notice as much as you can about them."

   ■ Even though the instructions didn't change, did your expectations and assumptions change the *second* time? the *third* time?

   ■ Based on the earlier experiences, you may have had specific expectations when the coleader took over. How did you feel when the coleader didn't behave as you anticipated?

   Did you feel angry, embarrassed, powerless, frustrated?

   Did you assume the coleader was wrong and didn't know how to play the game? What story did you have in your mind?

- What are the effects of expectations, assumptions, stories, and patterns in couple relationships?
- What are other similarities between this exercise and your relationships?

Sharing Halves

Because they each have equally important parts of the solution to navigating a maze, participants communicate and negotiate from a position of equal power and knowledge.

Goals

To improve communication.

To find a balance between sharing one's knowledge and listening to a partner's knowledge.

To practice negotiating in a context of equal power and knowledge.

Group size

2–20 participants.

Time

30 minutes.

Materials

Complementary mazes: **Labyrinth 1** and **2** worksheets; pencils.

Process

1. Ask participants to form two rows of chairs back-to-back, to select a partner of the opposite gender or a different culture, and to sit down with their back to that partner. If possible, make sure each pair includes either opposite gender or different cultures.

2. Provide the following instructions:

   ▪ In this exercise, you will each have half of the solution to navigating a maze. You need to find a balance between communicating the information that you have and listening to the information that your partner has.

   ▪ Since most of our communications are done in an environment of stress, I'm going to give you a time limit. You will have only 10 minutes to exchange as much information as you can and find the solution to this maze.

■ You need to find a constructive way of communicating, listening, and balancing the exchange of information so that both of you will be successful at the same time.

3. Distribute **Labyrinth 1** to participants facing in one direction, **Labyrinth 2** to those facing in the other direction. Then give the following instructions:

■ Imagine that you and your partner are lost separately in the same maze. Each of you has half of the information on where deadly mines are hidden.

■ I have given each of you the drawing of a maze. The walls are placed identically in both the mazes, but your maze shows only half the bombs, your partner's shows the other half.

■ You both want to exit the maze safely and need to share with each other your part of the information on the maze. How will you coguide each other out? Begin.

4. After 10 minutes, invite participants to compare their drawings, checking to be sure they didn't run into a bomb shown on either maze, and to reconvene in a circle for a discussion of the experience.

5. Lead a discussion using the following questions:

■ What was helpful in achieving this task?

■ What kind of problems interfered with efficiency?

■ What ways of communicating did you prefer?

■ How was the experience of each having equally important information to share?

■ How can that parallel the experience of dealing with conflicts in real life situations?

LABYRINTH 1

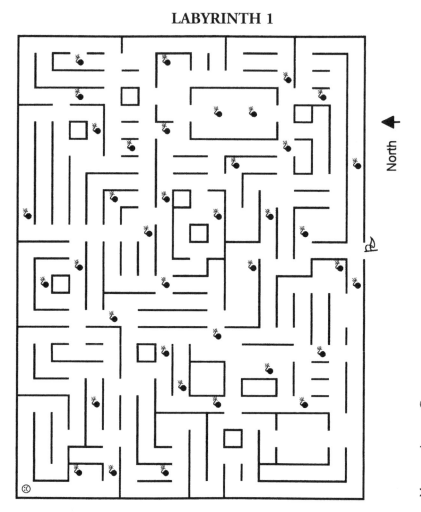

North

You are here ☺

LABYRINTH 2

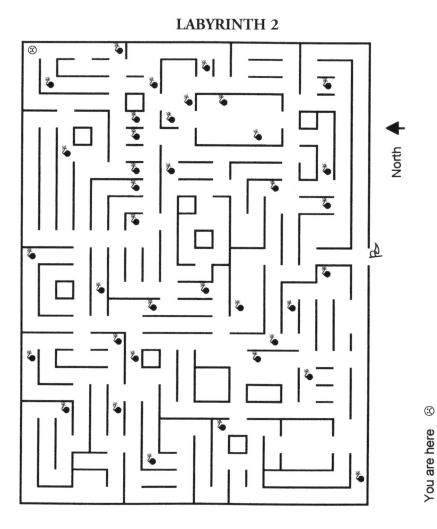

North

You are here ☺

Blind Obstacle Course

In this exercise, participants have the opportunity to cocreate an experience of trust and to explore different ways of communicating.

Goals

To practice being fully present while discovering senses other than visual and auditory.

To experiment with trusting a partner.

To practice nonverbal communication and support.

Group size

2–16 participants.

Time

45–60 minutes.

Materials

Bandannas to cover the eyes of half the participants; obstacles such as ropes, boxes, and wastebaskets; hula hoops; tape to create mazes on the floor; two pitchers of water and empty glasses for each participant.

☞ *Prior to the session, use masking tape to create two identical mazes. Add obstacles to step over and crawl through. Put pitcher and glasses at the end of the maze. Make sure your maze is safe.*

Process

1. Announce that this playful exercise will provide participants with the opportunity to practice communication at multiple levels: physical, directional, and emotional as they each guide a blindfolded partner through an obstacle course.

2. Underscore that guides should be very careful and conscious of their partners' dimension when going through a door or under

a rope for instance and be receptive to their partners' need for safety.

3. Divide the group in two equal teams and have participants form pairs.

4. Ask each team to stand behind their respective starting line (they each go through separate yet identical mazes).

5. Distribute the bandanas and provide the following instructions:
   - Ask your partner how he or she would like to be guided and held (by the waist, the hand, the shoulder).
   - Verify whether your partner is very trusting or prefers extra measures of care and safety, such as going slowly and getting a lot of instructions.
   - Provide as much verbal instruction as possible and minimize physical guidance, such as actually moving your partner's feet through the maze on the floor.
   - Your priority is not to win the race, but to communicate successfully and have a trusting experience with your partner. The reason this game is set up as a race is to add some time stress to your communication, not to practice competitiveness.
   - If you trip on a particular obstacle, touch the rope, or step on the tape on the floor and you feel that you ought to start over, restart only at that particular obstacle.

6. Once everyone has had a chance to experiment with both roles, have everyone applaud the group's effort and reconvene the entire group in a large circle.

7. Discuss the following questions:
   - What was your experience of this exercise?
   - What did you discover?
   - Was it harder to be blindfolded or to be a guide?
   - Was it difficult to trust?
   - What made it easier to trust your guide?

- How did your trust change throughout the exercise?
- What kind of communications were helpful?
- What was the most challenging aspect of the experience?
- How can you apply this experience in your life and your relationships?

Cooperation

This activity provides a playful way to begin the getting acquainted process. It also increases participants' awareness of how stories and assumptions about people may cause us to miss getting to know some wonderful people.

This activity is a perfect way to involve people as they are arriving for a program. Not only can it serve as an indirect way to begin the getting acquainted process, but it also allows people to notice the value of being different.

This exercise promotes equality in a relationship and requires partners to cooperate around the construction of a plan. It emphasizes how two individuals can be connected while respecting each others contributions and preferences.

This activity provides a laboratory for decision-making in a playful atmosphere.

In this exercise, participants playfully experience dealing with support and disagreements around the co-construction of a story.

This game is a variation of the "Emotion Mirror." It provides participants the opportunity to explore sharing the leadership of a physical dance.

This game is a fun, high energy activity in which participants share leadership and make physical decisions together that require an awareness of their partner's needs.

Actually . . .

This activity provides a playful way to begin the getting acquainted process. It also increases participants' awareness of how stories and assumptions about people may cause us to miss getting to know some wonderful people.

Goals

To increase our awareness about the thoughts and stories that we have about people when we first meet them.

To verify these stories.

To practice getting past first impressions and getting acquainted with the real person.

Group size

Up to 12 participants.

Time

15–20 minutes.

Materials

Actually . . . worksheet; pencils.

Process

1. Invite the participants to sit in a circle with someone they don't know on their right.

2. Give each person the **Actually** . . . worksheet and a pencil, then provide the following instructions:

   ■ Write your best guess about the person on your right's favorite cuisine, favorite type of music, and hobby or special interest. Make these guesses without talking to him or her. You will have 2 minutes to fill out the worksheet.

- Take turns introducing the person on your right as if he or she were your best friend. After you offer each guess, your partner will say: "Actually . . . " and give the real answer.

- For example, if I say, "This is my very best friend Kelly; her favorite cuisine is Italian and we love bungee jumping to-gether;" Kelly might respond, "Actually . . . my favorite food is chocolate ice cream and my hobby is painting."

3. Conclude the activity by asking participants to discuss some of the following questions:

  - How certain were you of your first impressions and stories about the person?

  - Have you noticed how your mind wanders, evaluates, judges, and creates stories about people you encounter?

    Why do you think it does that?

    When is it useful?

    When can it become problematic?

  - What can we do about these automatic and mostly insidious assumptions and judgments?

  - How do these stories affect relationships?

  - How can you protect yourself from the effect of these stories?

ACTUALLY . . .

The person on your right's first name: _____

Just by looking, make some assumptions about the person on your right. Base your guesses solely on your first impressions.

What is their favorite style of cuisine?

What is their favorite type of music?

What is their hobby or special interest?

Mystery Puzzles

This activity is a perfect way to involve people as they are arriving for a program. Not only can it serve as an indirect way to begin the getting acquainted process but it also allows people to notice the value of being different.

Goals

To recognize the benefit of having different perspectives on the same reality.

To notice how differences can assist in problem-solving situations.

To work with new people.

Group size

Unlimited; in groups of 2 or 3 participants.

Time

15–20 minutes.

Materials

Puzzle Page worksheet; pencils.

Process

1. Hand a **Puzzle Page** worksheet and pencil to each couple as they arrive (or assign 2 or 3 participants to small groups). Tell them to work together to solve as many puzzles as they can.

    ☞ *This game can be hard for people from other cultures, especially for those speaking a language other than English.*

2. After 15 minutes, move the group into one circle and invite participants to share solutions. Accept all alternative solutions. (Answer key is at the end of the exercise.)

3. Conclude the activity by asking participants to discuss the following questions:

- What was the experience like?

- Was working as a team helpful?

- Did your partners see a solution to some puzzles that you couldn't see initially? What was that like?

- What parallels can be drawn between this activity and your relationships?

- How would relationships be if we were all the same?

- Can you think of a time in your relationships where being different allowed for something positive to happen?

- What makes it so hard to deal with differentness?

- What strategies have you used in your relationships to deal with being different from each other?

- What are some of the advantages of people in relationships being different from each other? If the following aren't mentioned, add them to the list.

  more ideas for solutions when there are problems

  new discoveries and learnings

  different perspectives

ANSWER KEY

The plot thickens	Highway overpass	Bottom of the ninth
Scrambled eggs	Paradise	I understand
tricycle	Reverse discrimination	Quit following me

PUZZLE PAGE

On the lines below each sketch, write the word or phrase that it represents.

P **L O T**	way ___ pass	NINIH
gseg	*dice* *dice*	stand — I
cycle *cycle* *cycle*	noitanimircsid	**ME QUIT**

"Yes and . . ."

This exercise promotes equality in a relationship and requires partners to cooperate around the construction of a plan. It emphasizes how two individuals can be connected while respecting each others contributions and preferences.

Goals

To practice valuing and respecting differences.

To practice being open-minded and receptive.

To listen to and then acknowledge a partner's ideas.

To appreciate individuality and still create connectedness.

Group size

Unlimited.

Time

15–30 minutes.

Materials

Easel pad; markers (optional).

Process

1. Invite the participants to sit in chairs or on the floor facing a partner, with the pairs scattered around the room

2. Introduce the exercise, presenting the following information and offering your own examples where appropriate:

   ■ This exercise will give us practice in valuing and respecting other people's ideas, taking the time to acknowledge and find some value in each suggestion and opening ourselves to other ideas and perspectives.

   ■ We have all been well trained to look for what doesn't work;

therefore, we typically respond to novel ideas with "yes, but"—not even considering what may be of value in another person's idea.

- In the long run, this has the effect of narrowing our world down to only our own ideas and ways of doing things.

- "Yes and . . . " is a process that requires you to listen to what your partner says and acknowledge the value and the richness of each contribution.

- In this game, your goal is to plan a vacation that both partners will enjoy.

- To do this, you will take turns offering ideas, one at a time.

- After your partner offers an idea, you will respond by appreciating at least one aspect of what was offered.

- Use this phrase (you may want to write it on a flip chart or chalkboard): "What I like about your idea is . . . " completing it with something you can honestly say you like about the idea. Keep searching until you can find something you like.

- After offering your appreciation (which is the "Yes" step), you can say: "And . . . " add your own idea.

- In this exercise there are no restrictions whatsoever to limit your vacation. Budget, practicality, plausibility, possibility, and the laws of physics do not exist.

3. After 15 minutes of cocreation, conclude the exercise by asking participants to discuss some of the following questions:

- What was your experience of this exercise? Does anybody want to share where they ended up taking a vacation?

- How did it feel when your partner appreciated your ideas?

- Was it hard to always find something you appreciated about your partner's contribution?

- What effect did this attitude have on your participation?

- What effect did this attitude have on your vacation plan?

■ What effect might the "Yes, and . . . " attitude have on your relationships?

■ How would it be if everyone could hold on to this attitude in day-to-day interactions?

Team Decisions

This activity provides a laboratory for decision-making in a playful atmosphere.

Goals

To discover the decision-making process within a small group.

To explore gender differences in decision-making
To collaborate rather than compete

Group size

Four teams of 2–10 people.

☞ *If you are working with a small group of couples, see the note at the end of the exercise.*

Time

10–15 minutes.

Materials

None.

Process

1. Group participants in a standing circle. Ask for three suggestions of simple body positions that you identify as movements #1, #2, and #3. Review these positions at least twice to ensure that everyone remembers them.

2. Invite the participants to divide into three equal teams. If you want to focus on gender issues, you may want to have one all women, one all men, and the third mixed. Ask each team to stand together, forming one side of a triangle.

☞ *If you want couples to work together, form teams of 1–3 couples.*

3. Provide the following instructions:

- The goal of your team is to intuit which body position the other two teams will select so that the entire group will eventually take on the same position without the teams talking to each other.
- You will have 15 second to collectively decide on that position.
- When I say, "Begin," huddle together and decide.
- When I say, "1, 2, 3, Show," regroup into our triangle and assume the position your team has selected.

4. Begin the exercise, allowing one practice round. Reduce the amount of decision-making time with each turn.

5. When the entire group finally gets into the same position, conclude the exercise by asking participants to discuss some of the following questions:

- What strategies did their teams use?
- How was the position or movement chosen in your team?

  Was one person consistently the leader?

  Did others always follows?

  Did the decision making alternate between everyone in the team?

  Was the decision discussed?

- Was everyone listened to if they wished to share their idea?
- If two of the team members had different ideas, how did you negotiate the outcome?

  Does the same person make all the decisions?

  Is it equally important for everyone to have a turn to decide, or do some people not mind letting the others chose?

- How did this game parallel the decision-making process in your relationship?

Variation

If you want to have couples work together and thus will have more teams, take note of the following: The probability of success in this game is: *(# positions)* $^{\text{# teams-1}}$; in other words, if you have five couples, in order to have a decent probability of success it is advisable to have only two positions to choose from: *(2)* $^{5-1=4}$ = *16*. The group will probably achieve success in fewer than 16 attempts which is reasonable time-wise.

Good News, Bad News

In this exercise, participants playfully experience dealing with support and disagreements around the co-construction of a story.

Goals

To remain open during disagreements and differences.

To practice mental flexibility.

To expand the range of possibilities when confronted with obstacles.

Group size

Unlimited number of small groups, each with 3 or 5 participants.

Time

10–15 minutes.

Materials

Chairs, optional.

Process

1. Invite participants to sit on chairs or the floor in small circles of 3 or 5 players (must be an odd number) scattered around a room.

2. Ask for a volunteer from each group to be the starter.

3. Provide the following instructions:

   ■ Together, your team will create a story.

   ■ I will give you the first sentence; you will continue, each person adding a single sentence.

   ■ The first person's sentence must begin with the phrase, "The bad news was . . . " and continue with some kind of problem or disaster.

- The next player to the right starts the next sentence with, "The good news was . . . " and proceeds to turn that problem or disaster into a positive or adds a positive twist to the story. It is important to move the story forward by adding new information.

- As you take turns telling the story alternate "The bad news . . . " and "The good news . . . ".

- I will call time after 10 minutes. End your stories with a "The good news . . . ".

4. Discuss the following questions:

   - How did you experience the obstacles that were placed by your conarrators?

   - Did "frustration" get to you at times? How did it affect you?

   - Was it hard to let go of an idea or a goal for the story?

   - What did you like about the exercise?

   - Compare this process to developing a story by yourself. How do the processes differ?

   - Did you like the outcome of the story even if some of your contributions were modified by others?

   - Considering this process in the context of your relationships, what would be useful for you to remember?

Dance Mirroring

This game is a variation of the "Emotion Mirror." It provides participants the opportunity to explore sharing the leadership of a physical dance.

Goals

To explore the experience of letting go of control.

To share leadership.

To practice being receptive and sensitive to the needs of another.

Group size

Unlimited as space allows.

Time

10–15 minutes.

Materials

None.

Process

1. Invite participants to select a partner and stand facing that person, extending their arms forward, just touching fingertips to create a two-arms' length distance between them. Provide the following instructions:

   ▪ Decide which partner will be identified as A and which as B.

   ▪ Please refrain from talking until after the exercise.

   ▪ Partner A, begin a slow, fluid movement. Partner B mirror that movement exactly. Partner A, keep moving smoothly until I tell you to switch.

2. Switch the lead between A and B until participants establish a smooth comfortable rhythm.

3. Instruct participants to share the leadership and follow each other without having an identified leader.

4. Conclude the exercise by asking participants to discuss some of the following questions:
   - What was it like to mirror each other?
   - What was the difference between leading and following?
   - Which one was more comfortable?
   - Was it difficult to let go of some of your ideas?
   - How was it to share the leadership?
   - How does such a shared leadership apply to relationships?

Jail Escape

This game is a fun, high energy activity in which participants share leadership and make physical decisions together that require an awareness of their partner's needs.

Goals

To encourage participants to work as a team.

To practice taking care of each other while competing.

To respects each other's limitations.

Group size

Even numbers up to 24.

Time

10–15 minutes.

Materials

Chairs.

Process

1. Invite the participants to sit in a large circle consisting of chairs two by two, evenly spaced apart from other pairs. Two participants sit side by side in the center of the circle.

☞ *Note: If there is an odd number of participants, take one of the seats in the center of the circle so that you can demonstrate.*

2. Assign each pair a number (1, 2, 3, and so on) that will stay with them through the whole game. This number identifies their teams, not their chairs, which will constantly change.

3. Introduce the exercise with the following information:

   ■ Everyone is guaranteed a seat in this game; however there are two kinds of seats: preferred seats (indicating the outer circle of chairs) and jail (indicating the two chairs in the middle of the circle).

- If you are in jail, of course you want to escape. You get out of jail by calling a series of numbers, in any order, alternating between the two of you. The rules for calling numbers are: You must call at least three numbers and you cannot call your own. When you are finished calling numbers, one of the jail partners shouts "Go!"

- Upon the signal "Go!" all the pairs in the outer circle whose numbers have been called, get up and move quickly to other preferred seats, hoping to avoid going to jail.

- The pair that was in jail will also quickly look for preferred seats. The pair that remains standing must go to jail.

- To make things interesting, pairs will move as a unit with their arms interlocked at the elbows. (You may want to allow the pairs to practice maneuvering with their arms connected.)

- If at any time during the game, you become disconnected from your partner, go immediately to jail.

- Keep in mind: taking care of each other is a higher priority than getting preferred seats.

4. Use the first round of play for practice.

5. After several turns, offer a shortcut to move all the pairs at once: "Jail Break!" is the signal for everyone to "Go!" On "Jail Break!" pairs *cannot* move to the chairs on their immediate right or left. Remind the group that this signal will increase the need for taking care of each other.

6. End the game after a "Jail Break!" when everyone has been involved.

7. A discussion is optional after this exercise; however, if you want you may ask participants about their experience of nonverbal collaboration with some of the following questions:

- How did you and your partner quickly decide which way to go?

- How did you work with each other though you are different sizes, weight, and strength and move at different speeds?
- What was it like to balance the different goals of getting a chair (winning/the outcome) and taking care of your partner (playfulness/the process)?

Inspired by More New Games, *Headlands Press, 1981.*

Part 2

A Narrative Perspective

Unmasking Problems

Voices

Participants are invited to notice and bring forth the various inner voices that govern their life. The two main voices targeted in this exercise are the "critic" and the "ally."

Goals

To notice the different voices we experience.

To become aware of how they affect our lives and the meaning we ascribe to our experience.

To choose which voice is helpful and which should be disregarded.

Group size

Unlimited; groups of 3 or 4 participants.

Time

30 minutes.

Materials

None.

Process

☞ *Prior to the session, develop a list of situations to be used in step 5.*

1. Introduce the exercise with the following comments:
   - Most people experience their thinking as voices in their mind commenting on their experience. This is particularly the case when you feel ambivalent about something. A part of you says "yes, do it," another part of you says "no, don't." Similarly, when you doubt yourself, a part of you feels that you did the right thing and another part of you feels that you did not. It is helpful to view those as separate voices or external entities that you can observe from a distance and draw your own conclusions about what they "say."

- "Critical Voice" is a name that can be assigned to the critical and self-defeating thoughts that often cloud our mind when we struggle with bad feelings about ourselves.

- Critical thoughts are experienced as being derogatory to ourselves or our intimate partner. For example, they may take the form of negative statements such as "I can't believe I said that, that was stupid," "I'm so dumb," "I'm not good enough," "You did it on purpose," "You know how much I hate this," "You don't care" . . . and so on.

- The Critical Voice typically leads to negative feelings such as depression, anger, worthlessness, hopelessness, insecurity, anxiety, and distrust (to name only a few). It makes people feel awful about themselves and increases the conflicts and resentment in relationships.

- Many people experience these critical thoughts as a specific voice. Some people notice its presence without knowing where it comes from, while others report that it is their mother's voice, their father's, another family member's, or a teacher's. Often it is the voice of a well-meaning individual who simply wanted to teach something to you when you were a child but who inadvertently participated in the creation of the Critical Voice. Sometimes it comes from experiences of abuse. Identifying exactly where it came from is not so important as recognizing its effect in day-to-day life and making a conscious choice to silence it.

- Supportive people in your life may have helped you develop another voice: the voice of an Ally. Your Ally encourages you and takes a positive view of your actions and those of your partner.

2. Ask participants to sit as an audience and invite three volunteers to step forward (As the facilitator, you may chose to play one of the roles, in particular, the role of the Critical Voice). Clarify with the audience that one person, A, will do nothing but sit and listen to the battle of the voices while the two other volunteers

will play the role of the Ally, supportive and positive, and the Critical Voice, harsh and destructive.

3. When volunteers step forward, Person A is invited to sit down in a chair while the two others stand behind A, one by each shoulder to personify the two inner voices.

4. Repeat that in order to facilitate the process of the exercise, the inner voices are either 100 percent critic or 100 percent ally. Their role is to convince A of the validity of their views.

5. Once the volunteers are clear about their roles, specify the context of the scene. For example, a friend has just passed by A and completely ignored A's greetings. Ask participants portraying the two voices to comment on the situation. If they have trouble getting started, make a few of the following suggestions:

- Critic: He doesn't like you anymore;

- Ally: He probably did not see you;

- Critic: I'm sure he saw you but he didn't feel like talking to you, you're so boring;

- Ally: In the past he has always sought out your company so why would he deliberately ignore you;

- Critic: Remember last time you saw him, you made that completely stupid and inappropriate comment . . . you always do that and screw up relationships;

- Ally: It was not so bad, you're not even sure that it bothered him;

☞ *If the group consist of couples, use a relationship example that involves blaming a partner rather than self blame.*

6. You may conclude the exercise with the discussion at this point or elect to have each participant try these roles by forming groups of three.

☞ *Keeping the group together as an audience has the advantage of allowing audience members for whom this concept is completely new to reflect on it. Not everyone has had the opportunity to notice the different inner voices commenting on their experience. On the other hand, forming small groups allows everyone to practice different roles. This can be especially empowering for those people who experience an overwhelming "critic" and barely hear any "ally." This happens frequently to women or individuals who have been raised in an oppressive environment where the "critic" had a lot of support.*

7. Conclude the exercise by inviting people to share their experience. Ask them the following questions:

   ■ How were you affected by seeing the voice as an external entity?

   ■ Were you surprised by the statements it made?

   ■ How can this idea be helpful in your own lives and relationships?

   ■ What strategies can be used to fight the Critical Voice?

8. Invite participants to notice their Critical Voices during the week and pay attention to different ways of weakening it.

☞ *Increase the benefits of this exercise by moving immediately into the "Problem Interview" exercise, which begins on the following page.*

Problem Interview

This exercise, which should be used immediately after the "Voices" exercise, helps participants further understand the externalization of problems and deepens their understanding of blaming and critical voices.

Goals

To visualize and experience externalizing a problem.

To explore in depth a specific problem, such as blaming and critical voices.

To make more visible the insidious presence, actions, and patterns of problems.

Group size

Unlimited.

Time

30–45 minutes.

Material

Effects of Problems worksheet; pencils (facilitator may choose to wear a mask when personifying the Critical Voice).

Process

1. Since this exercise follows the "Voices" exercise, all participants should still be seated in a half circle or audience position.

2. Provide the following instructions:

   ■ Now that you have seen the Critical Voice in action, you will all be given the unique opportunity, the once in a lifetime chance, to interview this problem.

   ■ You may choose to ask all the questions that you've always wondered about such as: What is your goal? When are you most likely to attack people? Who or what supports you? How do you get people to believe in your criticism? What do you most like to do to make people feel bad? Do you criticize men and women in different ways? What kind of strategies can people use against you? . . . and so on.

3. If you have a cofacilitator, have that person initiate the interview as you personify the Critical Voice (preferably with a mask). Participants will usually warm up very quickly and engage in their own questioning.

4. When the group seems to run out of questions, announce that you will take one last question. After answering it, remove your mask if you wore one or physically change your body position while informing the group that you are becoming yourself again.

5. Engage participants in a discussion of their experience using the following questions:

   ■ What was your experience of this exercise?

   ■ What did you notice?

   ■ Could you recognize the influence of the Critical Voice in your life?

   ■ What did you discover about the problem?

   ■ Were you surprised by any of the questions or answers?

   ■ Do you think that the Critical Voice is often meaner in reality?

6. The role play demonstrated the benefits of externalizing a problem. Distribute the **Effects of Problems** worksheet and provide the following instructions:

   ■ The role play you just saw provided an example of externalizing a problem. Remember that people are not problems, they are dealing with a problem.

   ■ On your worksheet, externalize a problem that affects you. You will keep this sheet to yourself so your answers will be confidential. Imagine that it is outside of you or that it is an unhelpful habit that doesn't fit with the kind of person you want to be. You will have 5 minutes to complete this process.

7. Conclude with a discussion of the following question:

- How can externalizing be helpful in your own daily struggles or in your relationships?

Variation

After the group interview, you may ask participants to break into small groups of two or three and redo the exercise by themselves, playing the different roles of problem, interviewer, and (if three) observer or ally.

This exercise is adapted with permission from an original creation of Dr. Jeffrey Zimmerman and Dr. Victoria Dickerson of Bay Area Family Therapy Training Associates.

EFFECT OF PROBLEMS

Here are a series of questions that will help you apply this process to your own life. Name a problem that may be effecting you and answer the questions below by putting the name of the problem in the blank spaces. (example of problems: blaming, criticizing, withdrawing, anxiety, distrust, affectionism, self-doubt, anger . . .)

1. How does _____ affects you?

2. What does _____ make you:

   do?

   say?

   think?

   feel?

3. When and how did you first notice _____?

4. How does _____ affect your relationships? (Does it draw you closer or push you further apart?)

5. How does _____ make you feel about yourself?

EFFECT OF PROBLEMS (continued)

6. Does _____ make you do or say things that
you don't like to do? What kind of things?

7. When are you able to escape _____?

8. When are you most likely to resist _____?

9. What ideas are helpful to you in resisting _____?

10. How can a partner help in dealing with _____?

11. Based on your experience with _____ what advice would you
offer to other people struggling with _____?

©1998 Whole Person Associates 210 W Michigan Duluth MN 55802 (800) 247-6789

Problem-Ghost Congress

By personifying a problem that has affected their lives, participants broaden their understanding of the externalization of problems and separate themselves further from the influence of problems.

Goals

To deepen the understanding of externalizing problems.

To clearly separate problems from people.

To notice the influence of problems.

Group size

3–12 participants.

Time

60 minutes.

Material

Problem-Ghost Congress handout; **Problem-Ghost Script** worksheet; pens and pencils.

Process

1. Introduce the exercise with the following comments:

   ▪ Problems can be thought of as ghosts that take over a person's thinking, making them do or say things that they would not otherwise do or say. Problems get people to behave in ways they later regret and that don't fit with the kind of person they prefer to be. For that reason, it is helpful to treat them as external to you as ghosts that take over or as a virus that alters your state of mind.

   ▪ In this exercise, you will be invited to explore the personality of a problem that has affected your life. With the help of a worksheet, you can explore the behavior, attitude, and effects of this problem on yourself.

- You will then be invited to a Problem-Ghost Annual Congress at which each problem will be introduced and given the opportunity to present its harmful work to the group. Problems may choose to describe themselves, what they do to humans, and their meanest strategies. They can also ask the audience if anyone has any question on how to best accomplish that type of work.

2. Distribute the **Problem-Ghost Script** worksheet and the **Problem-Ghost Congress** handout. Give participants some time to complete the worksheet. As the master of ceremonies, go around the room and note the identity of each problem ghost since you will be introducing each of them later on when the gala begins. This is also a good opportunity to make sure that everyone understands the exercise and the process of externalization.

3. When everyone is ready, ask participants to sit in a row of chairs. Welcome them enthusiastically to the Problem-Ghost Congress, commending them for their fine work in making people miserable. Next, one after the other invite participants to come in front of the group to introduce themselves as if they were the problem ghosts and ask them to explain their work. Problem ghosts may simply read their script to the audience or act it out. Since the audience members themselves are problems, they should applaud profusely and cheer the performance of their problem peer.

4. When all participants have introduced themselves as a problem ghost, have them regroup in a circle and discuss the following issues.

- How was your experience of being a problem ghost?
- What effect did this exercise have on your attitude towards the problem?
- What was most surprising about your problem's personality?

- How differently will you react to this problem the next time it shows up in your life?
- How can seeing problems as external ghosts be helpful in relationships?
- What do you want to remember about this experience?

PROBLEM-GHOST CONGRESS!

Choose a problem that has affected you in your life. It can be anything such as an emotion (anger, anxiety, impatience, depression, frustration, self-hate, boredom, distrust, fear, shyness), a thought (critical voice, blaming, perfectionism, comparison, self-doubt, evaluation, ambition) or a habit or behavioral pattern (teasing, interrupting, dominating, rushing, irresponsibility, disrespect). Explore how this problem has affected you in the past and how you've seen it affect other people by completing the **Problem-Ghost Script**. Summarize the personality of the problem ghost in a few sentences that you will be comfortable reading to the group in the congress.

Example:

Hi, I am the critical ghost.

I like to be undercover and unnoticed. I wear camouflage clothing that blends me into the surroundings. People often think that I am a sneaky character because my power is at its highest when people are unaware of my presence. I typically stalk my victims and whenever they are alone, tired, or stressed out, I strike. I whisper in their ears that they were too spontaneous, stupid, wrong; I get them to focus on all the aspects of their day that didn't go as anticipated, to wonder about what others will think, and to imagine dreadful consequences to their behaviors. I drench them with guilt, shame, and worthlessness. I drool as my victim shrinks into a big black hole of self-hate and hopelessness. Because women often feel so imperfect, I love them; they are my favorite victims.

PROBLEM-GHOST SCRIPT

Hi, I am _____,

I like to _____
_____
_____

I am the kind of ghost who _____
_____
_____

Sometimes, people describe me as_____
_____
_____

I torture people by _____
_____
_____

I typically get them to think _____
_____
_____

I also make people feel _____
_____
_____

Then, they _____
_____
_____

I'm most happy when I succeed in _____
_____
_____

PROBLEM-GHOST SCRIPT (continued)

My favorite time to sneak in a person's head is when _____

_____

_____

I feel particularly strong when my victim _____

_____

_____

What supports me the most in my activity is _____

_____

_____

When no one stops me, I _____

_____

_____

Anger on Trial

By exploring with each other the effects of anger on their lives, participants clarify when and how anger is helpful or not, as well as its meaning in their relationship.

Goals

To increase participant's awareness of the effect of anger.

To clarify when anger is useful and when it isn't.

To understand what has influenced our perception of anger.

Group size

10–20 participants.

Time

1 hour.

Material

None.

Process

1. Introduce the exercise with the following information:

   - Recently a problem ghost named Anger was arrested for having potentially committed horrible crimes in the world.

   - You are among possible victims and have also been chosen to be on the jury.

   - You are gathering information and exploring what anger has done in your life and in the life of your loved ones.

   - Your goal is to talk to as many people and gather as much insight as possible about whether or not anger is guilty of some crimes.

2. Form two equal groups and ask one group to form a small circle facing outward. Ask the second group to form a circle around the first one facing inward so that each participant ends up looking at someone.

3. Provide the following instructions:

    ■ I will shout burning questions around anger's history, behavior, and effects, one by one.

    ■ You will talk to the person in front of you and answer the question as it applies to each of your lives. You will have 5 minutes to do so which means about 2 minutes for each of you.

    ■ When the time has elapsed, I will instruct one of the circles to move to the right or to the left so as to provide a new person to interview.

4. Start with the first question on the following list. After 5 minutes ask participants from the outer circle to move three to the left. Ask the second question. Once they have talked for 5 minutes, ask the inner circle to move two to the right, and so on until you've asked all the following questions:

    ■ How did anger affect your family?

    ■ Did anger affect your father and your mother in the same way?

    ■ What did anger get your parents to do or say?

    ■ How did anger make you feel as a child?

    ■ As an adult, how do you perceive anger now?

    ■ What does it mean to you when anger turns someone against you? Is it different when it's a man than when it's a woman?

    ■ What does it mean for a man to get angry? What does it mean for a women to get angry? Is it equally socially acceptable?

    ■ How do you feel as a man or as a woman when anger is directed at you?

    ■ When anger is around, what are you tempted to do? What do you prefer to do?

- Remember the last couple of time you felt frustrated, what kind of things did anger get you to think about the other person?

- What idea about anger do you find most helpful to hold onto as you try to be the person you prefer to be?

- Share a time when anger could have gotten you to be at your worst and you resisted it?

- Do you feel that anger has been a friend or an enemy in your life (or both)? Reach your personal verdict about whether anger should be found guilty.

5. Once all the questions have been asked, reconvene the group into a circle and ask each participant, one by one to state whether Anger was found to be guilty in their own lives and to justify their position.

6. Conclude the exercise by discussing the following questions:

- How did you experience this exercise?

- What were you most surprised by discovering?

- What did you notice about how anger affects each gender?

- When is anger helpful and when is it not?

- What strategies do people use to prevent anger from claiming their identity in a conflict?

- What would you like to remember from this game?

©1998 Whole Person Associates 210 W Michigan Duluth MN 55802 (800) 247-6789

Wanted

In this exercise, participants playfully develop a "Wanted" poster to actively express the externalization of a problem and their decision to challenge it.

Goals

Externalize the problem further in a concrete and playful way.

Create a written document that lists the effects (crimes!) of the problem.

Make a public declaration of resistance.

Group size

2–16 participants.

Time

30 minutes.

Materials

Wanted handout; blank **Wanted** worksheet; crayons.

☞ *This exercise should be done after the "Problem Interview" and the "Problem-Ghost Congress" exercises.*

Process

1. Explain to participants that if problems can be seen as ghosts that bring out the worst in people or make people engage in behaviors that they would rather not do, problems can also be seen as criminals.

2. Distribute the **Wanted** handout and the blank **Wanted** worksheet. Provide the following instructions:

   ■ I have given you a Wanted poster for the vicious criminal Self-Doubt.

- Read about his crimes, then think about one of the problems you confront and create a Wanted poster for it.

- When you are done, you will have the opportunity to share your poster with the group, but you may pass if you prefer.

3. Give participants about 15 minutes to fill out their handout and reconvene the entire group.

4. Ask for volunteers to make a public declaration against their problem criminal.

5. Facilitate a discussion around the following questions:

- What was it like to view the problem as a criminal?

- What was your reaction to writing its effect on your life as crimes?

- Was it hard to imagine how life would be without it (the reward)?

- What are the implications of reading your declaration out loud?

- Did this activity make you stronger or the problem stronger? In what way?

- How will this exercise affect your attitude towards the problem?

- Do any of you want to post this sign in your home?

©1998 Whole Person Associates 210 W Michigan Duluth MN 55802 (800) 247-6789

WANTED

NAME:

CRIME:

REWARD:

WANTED

This Community of Support has issued a search warrant against the following problem. Any information helpful in unmasking this dangerous criminal will be rewarded.

NAME OF CRIMINAL: *Self-Doubt*

CRIMES:

- enslaving and minimizing women's knowledge
- constantly comparing its victim with others "much better than her"
- evaluating negatively at all times and isolating
- paralyzing its victims with a "mind glue"
- replacing people's perceptions of their reality by other's views
- triggering acute episodes of anxiety and making decisions difficult
- requiring perfect accomplishments
- preventing people from trying and when they do, make them so nervous that they are very likely to fail

REWARDS:

peace of mind, more energy to focus on nurturing moments, self-confidence, success, meaningful connections, mindfulness

Teaming Up Against It

Participants have the opportunity to actually talk back to a problem (personified by another participant) with the assistance of an ally.

Goals

To further participants externalized view of the problem.

To allow them to practice talking back to the problem.

To experience the support of a team.

Group size

3–20 participants.

Time

1 hour.

Material

Masks are helpful for the participants playing the problem. Otherwise participants sometimes refuse or feel guilty to take on harsh problem voices.

Process

1. Form small groups of 3 or 4 participants.

2. Provide the following instructions:
   - You will now have the opportunity to actually talk back to problems.
   - One member of your group will play the role of a problem chosen by another member, person A, who wants to stand up to this specific problem.
   - The person playing the role of the problem will be identified by wearing a mask.
   - The member who actually chooses the problem, person A,

will give the problem-person one or two sentences to repeat over and over again. For example, if I am asked to play "Doubt" as a problem, I will also be given by the member of the group who wishes to fight doubt (person A) one or two sentences such as: "You really can't trust anyone," and "You are just worthless." It is important that the problem person does not add any of their own statements. This exercise can make people feel vulnerable so it is critical to respect their limits and the specificity of what they already have tackled.

- As the role play progresses, the problem person will repeat these sentences over and over again, allowing person A to find many replies to these statements.

- The other members of the subgroup play the role of allies or teammates. They assist person A in finding replies to the problem's statements but only when person A makes eye contact with them thus indicating a desire for help.

3. Allow 5 minutes per person per role. Remind participants to switch roles every 5–7 minutes.

4. Discuss the effects of this exercise on participants perceptions of their ability to resist problems in their everyday life. People typically find this exercise extremely empowering and are very eager to talk about their experience. If the group is very large, it may be helpful to have them debrief the experience within their own little subgroup.

Autobiography of a Talent

Participants write the story of one of their special talents, specifically one that they use to stand up to a problem.

Goals

To invite participants to recognize some of their resources.

To increase their awareness of their ability to make changes in their lives.

To allow them to recognize the history of their talent and perhaps connect it to meaningful people in their lives.

Group size

2–26 participants.

Time

30 minutes.

Material

Autobiography of My Talent worksheet; pencils.

Process

☞ *At this point in the group or workshop, participants should have a clear understanding of the problem and its effect and should have recognized some instances when they were able to successfully combat the problem by using certain strategies.*

1. Invite participants to reflect on what it is about them that allows them to face the problem and make different choices in difficult situations.

2. Distribute the **Autobiography of My Talent** worksheet and pencils and provide the following instructions:

   ■ You will now have the opportunity to write the autobiography of your talent.

- If, for example, determination has helped you make changes in your life, you could write about:

  How determination might have developed during your childhood

  What made it grow stronger

  Who, in the past has seen this determination and how they came to discover it

  Who, in the present knows about this talent

  When it is most visible

- Before you begin the worksheet, listen while I read a sample autobiography called Story of Courage.

  > My courage first came to me when I was still a very young child. It emerged out of my hard determination to survive oppression, unfairness, pain, and confusion. Courage would not let me die despite the starvation and the injuries. Courage gave me hope, reminded me of my dream, and provided a wonderful little paradise in my mind.

  > As I grew older, courage made a warrior out of me. It made me escape into my studies and win, reach out for friends and find love, try activities and discover pleasure.

  > Yet it took me many years to acknowledge It, see It, and recognize It. Somehow I hadn't noticed all It's silent support until recently . . . when others pointed It out to me. Courage has now become older but It's wisdom still shines. I now cherish It and nurture It as much as I can. It is my best friend and It lives within me.

3. Now ask participants to write their autobiography of a talent on their worksheet.

4. When everyone has finished, ask participants to read their document to the group if they are comfortable sharing it.

5. Discuss what they discovered about themselves through this exploration.

AUTOBIOGRAPHY OF MY TALENT

Choose a special talent that you have and by filling in the following blank spaces, explore your past, present, and future experiences of it. (Examples of these can be: patience, courage, wisdom, inner strength, determination, self-confidence, thoughtfulness, compassion, etc.)

I first discovered _____ when

I realized it allowed me to

If I hadn't _____ I would

Having _____ made it possible to

Now that I know that I have _____ I will

The people in my life who have most supported _____ are

They did so by

I think that they knew about _____ because they noticed

Appreciation Bombardment

Participants interview each other about aspects of themselves they appreciate. They are acknowledged by the group for those preferred aspects of themselves.

Goals

To bring forth participants' preferred aspects of themselves in a public forum.

To allow participants to get to know each other on a meaningful level.

To allow participants to experience appreciation from their peers for their preferred aspects of themselves.

Group size

2–20 participants.

Time

30 minutes.

Material

Preferred Self worksheet; pencils.

Process

1. Welcome participants to the session. Then distribute the **Preferred Self** worksheet and pencils, then provide the following instructions:

   ■ When people struggle with problems, other aspects of themselves are often forgotten.

   ■ In this exercise, you will have the opportunity to make those aspects more visible and share your special talents with the group.

- You will have 15 minutes to discover one meaningful thing about as many people as you can and write it down on your worksheet.

- You may approach each other by asking about a special talent, an accomplishment, an experience, a hobby they are good at, or a challenge they've been able to realize.

- When you are being interviewed, provide different information to each interviewer.

2. After 15 minutes invite the group to make a sitting circle. Ask a volunteer to give his or her name. Then, one by one, each of the interviewers who have information about this person should stand up and share it with the group. End with a round of applause for each person.

3. When everyone has been acknowledged, discuss participant's experiences of this exercise and how they felt about being acknowledged.

PREFERRED SELF

Instructions for interviewers: Interview as many people as you can. Introduce yourself to an interviewee and find aspects that you didn't know about them (either a personal or job-related skill, accomplishment, task, or contribution they feel good about). Record what each person tells you in the space below their name.

Instructions for interviewee: Share briefly something that you are proud of about yourself with each interviewer. Once something about you has been written down, do not include that piece of information in any other interview.

Information you provide will be shared with the whole group.

Name: _____

_____

_____

Name: _____

_____

_____

Name: _____

_____

_____

Name: _____

_____

_____

Name: _____

_____

_____

Lifting Problem-Cloaks

In this closing exercise, participants visualize how problems are like dark cloaks that blind us to our potential and abilities. Each person is invited to engage in a ritual, lifting a problem-cloak to allow a light to shine.

Goals

To visualize the effect of problems on our personality.

To separate our potential from the effect of problems.

To create a community of support to fight problems.

To make a public commitment to our preferred way of being.

Group size

3–10 participants.

Time

15 minutes + (2 minutes x number of participants)

Materials

A small lamp with a low wattage bulb; a scarf, bandana, or piece of fabric for each participant. Be careful that the lamp will not set a fire.

Process

1. Ask participants to form a tight circle of chairs or to sit on the floor close to each other. Place the lamp in the middle of the circle, light it, and close all other sources of light. Verify that everyone is comfortable with such a low light. Introduce the exercise with the following information:

   ■ As we have seen in previous exercises, problems can be seen as ghosts, viruses, or external entities that prevent us from being at our best.

- We will now visualize how problems effect us by imagining that they are like a cloak or a heavy piece of material that prevents us from seeing clearly. In other words if our unique potential as individuals is like a light, the problem is like a cloak interfering with the light's full potential to shine.

2. Distribute a piece of fabric to each participant and ask them to mentally complete the following two sentences:

"(problem) has prevented me from _____.
By lifting this cloak I commit to myself to remember that I can escape its influence by trying to _____this week ."

3. Provide the following example:

"Shyness has prevented me from talking to new people. By lifting this cloak I commit to myself to remember that I can escape its influence by holding on to my determination and trying to talk to a new person this week."

4. When everyone is ready, have each participant one by one place their piece of material on the lamp, make their statement and then remove the piece of material. It is often helpful for the facilitator to start to set the tone with a personal example.

5. When everyone has had a chance to share their statement, invite them to stand up and place an arm on each of their neighbors' shoulders to form a group hug. End with everyone applauding the group's commitment.

This exercise was inspired by one of Marie-Nathalie Beaudoin's students at John F. Kennedy University: Charlotte Davis.

Stories and Effects

By becoming aware of their thinking, participants are invited to notice how people organize what they see and experience into a story and how these stories have implications and effects on the actions they take. Participants are invited to notice the multiplicity of possible narratives around each lived experience.

Goals

To notice in a playful way how we story all lived experience.

To become aware of the effects of certain stories.

To notice how we make meaning of our experience.

To invite participants to remember to explore a broader range of stories.

Group size

10–20 participants.

Time

30 minutes.

Materials

None.

Process

1. Present the following introductory comments:
   - People tend to organize their lived experience into stories.
   - The stories that we develop include some information and exclude other because our life experience is much richer than what we can actually narrate.
   - However, the stories we choose to believe have many implications in our lives, our actions, our thoughts, and our feelings.

- Let's explore this process by acting as witnesses to an emotional scene.

2. You may choose to perform the scene with a cofacilitator or ask for two volunteers to perform in a 1 minute scene. If you choose to use volunteers, whisper to each of them the sentence they each are to say and the corresponding emotional expression they need to express. An example of a possible scene is:

Participant #1 (crying and yelling): "Let me go, let me go."

Participant #2 (in an angry tone of voice): " I will not let you leave."

3. Ask the other participants, one after the other, to share their guess or story about what happened and to speculate on what action they would take based on their story. (Acknowledge that we all know that these are only first impressions.)

4. Present two or three scenes and then move into a discussion.

5. Discuss the following questions:
   - What did you notice about your perception of one-minute scenes.
   - Did you find yourself creating a story?
   - Did you find yourself paying attention to certain things and not others?
   - Did your mind try to organize what it was seeing in a logical sequence of events?
   - Did you find yourself filling the holes in the story by developing explanations that were consistent with the story line you chose?
   - Does anyone know where their bias came from? For example, since I work with battered women, my initial assumption could be that this women is trying to escape an abusive partner. Others can think #2 is preventing #1 from running away or that #2 found #1 stealing. There are a huge number of possible stories that we can create.

- What do think affected the stories that came to your mind? We are all biased by important filters in our life experience: anything from a TV show you saw last night where a women wanted to attempt suicide (and her friend tried to hold her back) to a difficult situation you have lived yourself.

- How do these stories affect the meanings we make out of our life?

- How do these stories affect us when we deal with conflicts in relationships?

- What kind of problems can stories invite? Do we have stories about people's intentions in conflict?

- How will remembering this exercise affect your life and your relationships?

6. Conclude by saying that what is important to remember is that life is much bigger than these stories; life offers many more possibilities. It is the nature of the brain to make assumptions, we can't really change that, but we can learn to recognize these thoughts as only hypotheses or stories and not truths.

Variation

Have the group sit in front of a chalkboard. Invite participants to think of the way people in general would respond to a situation such as "your partner is two hours late for supper." The facilitator writes those responses in a column on the chalkboard. When everyone has exhausted the list of possible statements, invite them to share what stories they created about the situation that led them to choose those particular responses. In other words, invite people to share how they came up with those statements. When all the stories and assumptions are shared, add more information about the situation at hand (for example, the partner may have had an accident or ran out of gas) and invite people to reflect on how that would change their stories and their responses.

Conflict Simulation

Beginning with a series of vignettes, participants work as partners to explore typical conflicts and discover new ways to interact.

Goals

To discuss gendered ways of dealing with conflicts.

To externalize conflicts.

To generate solutions.

Group size

Unlimited pairs.

Time

1 hour.

Materials

Vignettes handout; easel pad and markers.

Process

1. Introduce the exercise by offering the following information:

   - We will explore conflict resolution by paying attention to our usual way of dealing with situations and the effects of our words and actions.

2. Demonstrate the exercise with your cofacilitator or with a participant by choosing one of the vignettes and escalating the conflict.

3. Ask participants to select a partner or have life partners work together. Invite each pair to randomly join another pair so that each couple can alternate from actors to spectators.

4. Distribute the **Vignettes** handout and provide the following instructions:

- Here is a list of vignettes that present typical conflicts that can occur between partners. Choose one of these examples that is meaningful, challenging, or relevant to you. If you and your partner cannot agree on which example to explore, do the activity around the difficulty of making this decision.

- When each pair has chosen their vignette, one pair starts by acting their sketch and takes a few minutes to argue about this situation as they would normally do or as they believe a typical couple would. Try to make your arguments as close as possible to your own experience even if that means moving away from the vignette.

- When this first pair is done, ask the second pair to act their vignette while the first pair watches.

- Pay attention to the effects of your statements, whether they seem to have a helpful or unhelpful effect.

5. After approximately 10 minutes, invite participants to discuss what they noticed, what worked, and what was not helpful. It is often helpful to write the comments on an easel pad in two columns, one listing unhelpful elements and the other listing helpful skills to remember.

6. Continue by presenting another vignette with your cofacilitator or a participant. The first time, act in a typical way (blaming, criticizing, assuming bad intentions). The second time, repeat the vignette in a constructive way (externalizing the problem and focusing on helpful attitudes).

7. Invite participants to rediscuss their conflict by selecting one of the discussed strategies, one that fits for them, one that they are less familiar with, and trying to apply it to their vignettes. In particular, invite participants to externalize a problem that is affecting the resolution of their conflicts (for example, anger or distrust). You may explain this in the following way:

- Each of you may try to find an externalization that reflects your experience of the problem and share with your partner how it affects you, explore how it affects them, and what it means for each of you.

8. After approximately 10 minutes, ask participants if any team would like to demonstrate a new way of responding to the conflict in their vignette.

9. Conclude the activity by asking participants to discuss their experience.

VIGNETTES

1. A woman is involved in an activity such as reading or watching TV. Her partner sneaks quietly behind her and surprises her. She angrily shouts: "I told you I hate it when you do that."

2. A man and a woman have had an argument in the morning, and the man walked out the door while his partner was still talking. He comes home at the end of the day with a bouquet of flowers which his partner angrily throws in the garbage.

3. A man announces to his partner that he accepted an invitation for both of them for dinner at their neighbor's home for the next evening. They both end up angrily discussing when it's appropriate to consult each other about activities. The women is furious.

4. A woman relates to her husband the conflict she had with her boss, and the man eagerly offers solutions. Both of them become increasingly frustrated as the conversation progresses.

5. A woman feels that her partner doesn't care enough for her and gets furious when she pursues activities by herself.

6. A man is annoyed by his partner's desire to be involved in the relationship only if it remains open and uncommitted.

7. A couple argues as to whether spaghetti should be cut or not before cooking them.

8. A couple argues as to whether the person who cooks should also do the dishes or not (they alternate the responsibility of cooking).

9. A person wants to go out with friends alone on a Saturday night, and his partner feels excluded.

10. A night owl and an early bird are trying to plan a date together.

11. A couple has some financial difficulties. One of the partners wants to buy something that seems unreasonable to the other.

12. A couple argues about the logistics of their next vacation.

13. One partner of a couple desires to get married and the other is reluctant to do so. They have been dating for two years.

Word Awareness

This game invites participants to pay attention to words that they find unhelpful in their communications or words that signal the presence of a problem-ghost.

Goals

To increase awareness of the choice of words, their implications, and their effects.

To notice to which extent certain words are used, even when a conscious attempt is made to avoid them.

Group size

4–10 participants.

Time

20 minutes.

Materials

None.

Process

1. Invite participants to make a circle of chairs or divide the group into groups of 4 or 5 participants.

2. Give the following explanations:

   ■ As we have experienced in the previous games, some words promote problems, conflict, and distress. Words like "you," "but," and "should" may invite blaming or critical voices and may lead relationships into conflict.

   ■ Each person's experiences are different, so words may affect people in various ways. A word that has a negative connotation for one person may be positive for another.

- In this game, we will practice noticing the use of unhelpful words and make a conscious effort to avoid them.

3. Ask participants to choose three unhelpful words they would like to become more aware of. In this facilitative process, we will call these "taboo" words. Make sure that participants choose words that they have personally experienced as unhelpful as opposed to you choosing the words for them.

☞ *Participants often discover these taboo words in the "Conflicts in Relations" exercise.*

4. Stand in the center of the circle and continue with the following instructions:

- Because I don't like standing in the middle of the circle without a chair, I will try to get back in the sitting circle by tricking someone into saying the taboo words during a casual discussion.

- Everyone else must pay a careful attention to the answers of the interviewee and signal any mention of the taboo words. If the interviewee mentions one of those words, he or she will have to give me a chair and come in the middle of the circle.

- The person in the middle is allowed to use any words they want.

5. Model the activity by randomly talking to anyone of your choice and trying to get them to say the taboo words. You can move from one participant to another when asking questions. Once a participant uses any one of the three words, take his or her chair. Continue the game for 15 minutes.

6. Conclude by asking participants to comment on their experience of the exercise. You can ask the following questions:

- What did you discover in this exercise?

- Were you surprised to hear yourself saying words you consciously were trying to avoid?

- How do you explain this?

- Was it hard to notice other participants saying those words?

- How do you explain that even though the whole group is listening, sometimes only one person notices that these words were said?

- What does this exercise imply in terms of communicating in relationships?

- When those words are used in a conversation, what effect do they have on you?

- How do you prefer to be talked to?

Options Walk

In this active exercise, participants explore the different possibilities around doing a simple task. The result is a greater appreciation for each other's ideas and an awareness of how we are socially shaped and trapped into narrow ways of being.

Goals

To expand the possibilities around doing a simple task.

To support and encourage each participant's unique ideas.

To discover that there are many perspectives to any problem or situation.

Group size

8–15 participants.

Time

3–45 minutes.

Materials

Masking tape.

Process

1. Invite participants to stand in a line, side by side, on one side of the room.

2. Inform them they will be assigned a simple task. The goal of the exercise is to see how many different ways they, as a group, can do this task.

3. Announce that there are only three rules:

   ■ Each person will contribute an idea individually;

   ■ Each contribution will be different from everything already done;

- Every contribution will be appreciated and enthusiastically supported by the group.

4. Have the group review the three rules. Remind them that those are the only three rules.

5. Describe the task:

   - Start here (put a masking tape X on the floor about 3 feet into the room from the head of the line of participants) and end up here (put another masking tape X on the floor about 10 yards away from the first X at a slight angle away from the line of people—see diagram).

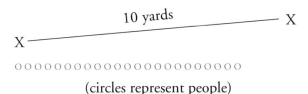

(circles represent people)

   - Your task is to find an original way to move from the first X to the second X.

   - When you arrive at the second X, the whole group will enthusiastically express their appreciation.

6. Go first to give an example (do something simple, like walk), making sure that the group enthusiastically appreciates you when you reach the second X.

7. Invite the next person at the beginning of the line to go from the first to the second X and encourage the group to enthusiastically applaud them.

8. Allow each person to have at least three or four chances to participate.

9. Conclude the exercise by asking participants to discuss some of the following questions:

   - What did you discover in this exercise?

- Were there more "solutions" than you initially thought of?

- What allowed people to find so many ways of doing the task?

- Did you notice any extra rules you had been operating with? (A good clue to an extra rule is when you hear your mind say: "I didn't know you could do that.")

- How does this exercise parallel day-to-day experiences of problems?

- What strategies do you each use to not let problems such as hopelessness, depression, or frustration narrow your choices and limit your possibilities?

- How can the ideas discussed in this exercise be useful in a relationship?

- How are these ideas relevant to cultural or gender differences?

Individuality
and Connectedness

Gender Quiz

In this exercise, which uses a game show format, participants are invited to reflect on facts and statistics related to gender issues, stereotypes, and privileges.

Goal

To increase participants' awareness of gender differences.

Group size

12–20 participants.

Time

1 hour.

Materials

A bell that is safe to use in a context where people run and jump.

Process

1. Divide the group into two teams with an equal number of men and women on each side.

2. Provide the following instructions:

   ■ In this game, I will read a list of questions on gender issues. You will have 30 seconds to discuss and agree on your team's answer to each question.

   ■ When I say go, a representative of the team must run to the bell in the middle of the room and reach it before a representative of the other team.

   ■ The first team to reach the bell must ring it and share the answer they've come up with.

   ■ If the answer is right, you win the other teams' representative. If the answer is wrong, the other representative gets to state their answer and, if it is correct, win you.

- The game will go on until one team "eats up" the other team or until all the questions have been answered.

3. Explain briefly each answer as it is presented. This is a high energy game and participants typically laugh and run a lot. Make sure to remind people to take care of themselves and of each other.

4. Conclude with a general discussion of the statements that surprised them the most.

GENDER QUIZ QUESTIONS

Which gender feels more entitled to have opinions and be right? (male)

What percentage of obese women have been sexually abused? (35%)

Which group has the highest self-esteem in general, African American women, Asian women, Latino women or white women? (African American)

What percentage of women are dissatisfied with how their body looks? (97%)

What percentage of men are dissatisfied with how their body looks? (30%)

What is the main reason for men to have a penile enlargement? (looks for locker room and dating situations)

Which gender has to wait 72 hours before being biologically able to have an orgasm after age 70? (Men)

The word misogyny means hate women; which word means hate men? (doesn't exist)

When a couple does not want to have kids anymore, which is the easiest surgical procedure? (vasectomy)

In the U.S., a women is raped every how much time? (3 minutes)

What is the number one regret than men have on their death bed? (having spent too much time working instead of with their loved ones)

On average, for equal education, experience, qualification, and job description, how much less does a women earn? (20–30%)

How many women die as a result of unhealthy dieting or anorexia every year in the U.S.? (1,500)

Which respective aspect of gender roles gets in the way of gay and lesbian relationships? (men: difficulty with commitment; women: expecting high levels of nurturing and sacrifice from their partners)

This exercise was adapted from one of Louise Yolton Eberhardt's activities in her book entitled Bridging the Gender Gap *published by Whole Person Associates.*

©1998 Whole Person Associates 210 W Michigan Duluth MN 55802 (800) 247-6789

Merging Stories

Participants co-construct a single story of their lives as if they were one person. Through this process, they notice how rich and diverse each person's experience has been, how their stories do not encompass all of their lived experience, how we naturally narrate our lives as stories, and how stories are co-constructed in relationships and interactions.

Goals

To notice to which extent people's lives are shaped differently by their sociocultural environments.

To make visible the process of experiencing our lives as stories.

To notice how being in a relationship involves coauthoring a joint story.

To deepen intimacy and connectedness by allowing participants to share historically important events in their life.

Group size

Unlimited.

Time

45–60 minutes.

Materials

None.

Process

1. Ask participants to pair with a partner with whom they feel comfortable sharing aspects of their life experience.

2. Provide the following introduction:

   ■ Everyone typically has a story of their life based on certain significant events or experiences that are tied together in a linear sequence. Our lived experience is much richer then this story we tell.

■ How do we determine which events we include in our story and which ones we don't? Events that we remember and include in our narrative are typically the ones that have involved interaction with others. In that sense we can say that our stories of ourselves are co-constructed.

■ In this exercise, you will be invited to co-construct a story by merging aspects of each of your lives into one single story.

■ Through this process, I would also like to invite you to notice how differently you have been shaped by your social environment. If it feels comfortable, feel free to include a statement about the social discourses or the contextual constraints that affected that particular experience, e.g. patriarchy, poverty, class, heterosexual dominance.

■ When I ask you to begin, one person will start by making a short one or two sentence statement about their birth, then the other person will make one or two statements about an event in their first year of life, then the first person will continue with a statement about their second year and so on. This alternating process would give a listener the impression that it is one person telling the story.

3. It is often helpful to give an example with your cofacilitator. For example:

Participant 1: When I was born, my mother was so shamed by her religious community that she had to place me for adoption.

Participant 2: When I was one years old, my parents moved to San Francisco because my father's job was relocated.

Participant 1: When I was two years old, I fell on the floor and broke my leg. We couldn't afford the surgery I needed to fully recover.

©1998 Whole Person Associates 210 W Michigan Duluth MN 55802 (800) 247-6789

4. Remind participants to make only one or two statements during each turn. People typically enjoy this process so much that they tend to elaborate on each event.

5. When half of the group is done, instruct others to wrap up within the next 5 minutes and ask the ones who are done to discuss their experience of the exchange with everyone.

6. Conclude with a discussion of their experience and of the following questions:

   ■ What was it like to coauthor a single story?

   ■ What did you notice about your own storying process?

   ■ Were you surprised by the level of differences and similarities in your lives?

   ■ Did you become aware of any privileges you may have had that your partner didn't have?

   ■ How are your behaviors, emotions, and thoughts affected by the stories you tell of yourself?

   ■ How can that knowledge of your mutual stories affect your relationships?

   ■ With couples: Are you now understanding aspects of your partner's life that were confusing to you before?

   ■ With couples: How do you think your intimate relationship is affected by these different life stories?

This exercise was adapted from a birthday ritual created by Michele Rousseau, Marie-Nathalie Beaudoin's mother-in-law. At every birthday party, she invited family members to alternate in sharing something about each year of the honored child's life as the candles were blown out one by one. When she had twin girls, she eventually had her two daughters alternate saying something they remembered of each other's life, year by year as they blew out the candles one by one.

Contextual Distances

By moving physically in the room, participants increase their awareness of how different contexts, privileges, and experiences have shaped them and how those experiences can create distance between people.

Goals

To become aware of privileges and different life experiences.

To notice the different contexts that shape people's lives.

To visualize the distance that might be experienced in relationships because of different contextual backgrounds such as race, ethnicity, socioeconomic status, divorce, etc.

Group size

Unlimited.

Time

45 minutes.

Materials

List of contextual differences items.

Process

1. State the exercise's goals, then ask participants to form one row, standing side-by-side in the middle of the room. Provide the following instructions:

   ■ I will read a series of statements that may or may not apply to your life experience.

   ■ When a statement touches your experience, I will invite you to either take a step forward or a step backward.

   ■ As this exercise will involve some self disclosure, please feel free to ignore the indication to move if it doesn't feel comfortable or safe to do so. It is important to take care of yourself.

2. One at a time, read the list of statements provided at the end of this exercise, pausing between each statement to allow people to move.

3. When all the statements have been read, ask participants to notice where they stand relative to everyone else.

4. Ask participants to choose someone they feel is very different from them and share their experience of the exercise. Allow 5 minutes for this process.

5. Ask participants to choose someone who they believe had similar experiences or who they can trust and discuss the "step" that was most meaningful, risky, or surprising for each of them. Allow 5 minutes for this process.

6. Reconvene participants in a circle and discuss the general effects of privilege and lack of privilege on individuals. Once participants have a good picture of these issues, discuss how such contextual differences may affect relationships in preferred as well as unwanted ways. You can also more specifically discuss the following questions:

   ■ Overall, how were you affected by this exercise?
   ■ Was it hard or easy to take the steps?
   ■ Were you sensitive to the movement of the group?
   ■ How did you feel when you were the only one moving or not moving?
   ■ Did you notice certain privileges that you have and that you had never been aware of before? How did that affect you?
   ■ Are you surprised to discover the variety of experiences in the group?
   ■ How can an awareness of these contextual differences be helpful in relationships?

Variation

If your group consist of couples, invite participants to notice where their partner stands relative to their position throughout the exercise. At the end, invite them to regroup and share with each other their experience of noticing these differences. You can more specifically discuss the following questions:

- How did the distance affect you?
- Were you aware that your partner had been exposed to these life experiences?
- What does that make you feel, think, or understand about your relationship?
- Is there anything you will want to explore further with your partner or anything you will want to do differently now that you have become aware of these experiences?

CONTEXTUAL DISTANCES

If you have three siblings or more, take a step forward.

If your parents still live together, take a step back.

If your life has been endangered at some point in time, take a step forward.

If your parents owned your home when you were young, take a step back.

If your parents each came from a different socioeconomic background, take a step forward.

If religion affected your life as a child in a more positive way, take a step back; in a more negative way, take a step forward.

If you worked before the age of eighteen, take a step forward.

If, when you were young, you had friends of color, take a step forward.

If you didn't knew someone who was gay when you were a teenager, take a step back.

If a member of your family has had a relationship with a partner from a different culture, take a step forward.

If when you were young, you could have been arrested for an act you did, take a step forward.

If you have been arrested in your life, whether or not you actually committed a crime, take a step forward.

If you never have had surgery or a major health problem, take a step back.

If a close relative has not died, take a step back.

If you worked your way through college, take a step forward.

If you never worried about having enough food to eat as a child, take a step back.

If you worried about being able to provide for yourself or your family as an adult, take a step forward.

If one of your close relatives had struggles with alcohol, take a step forward.

If you have hated your body, take a step forward.

If you've experienced people regularly distrusting you because of how you look, in stores, for example, take a step forward.

If you have been uncertain of your sexual orientation, take a step forward.

If you currently have friends who are gay or are members of any marginalized group, take a step forward.

If your mother had access to as much money as your father, take a step back.

If there was some abuse in your family, take a step forward.

If you were often physically hit or abused as a child, take a step forward.

If you were a victim of violence as an adult, take a step forward.

If you were never really close to either of your parents, take a step forward.

If your father took the time regularly to engage in activities with you as a child, take a step back.

If you have never tried drugs in your life, take a step back.

If one of your close relatives suffered from an incapacitating illness, take a step forward.

If you have worried about losing a parent, take a step forward.

If you suffered from being adopted or placed in foster families, take a step forward.

If you moved at least three times as a child, take a step forward.

If you were popular as a kid, take a step back.

If you have never traveled outside of the U.S., take a step back.

Gender Dream

This exercise invites people into the opposite gender's experiences. It increases participants' awareness of gender stereotypes, roles, privileges, and restraints.

Goals

To increase participants' awareness of gender differences.

To provide an experiential perspective on social restraints and privileges associated with gender trainings.

Group size

Unlimited.

Time

45–60 minutes.

Materials

Gender Differences and Stereotypes worksheet; pencils.

Process

1. Share the goals of the exercise and provide the following instructions to participants:

   ■ Lean back in your chair or find a comfortable place to lie down.

   ■ When you are ready, close your eyes. I will lower the lights. Raise your hand if you are not comfortable with me doing that.

   ■ Breathe slowly and deeply, in . . . and out . . . in . . . and out . . . Relax and become ready to use your imagination, to visualize and add details to the scene I am about to describe.

2. Continue by reading the following script, allowing plenty of time for participants to imagine each scene.

Imagine that during your sleep, a genie has played a trick on you, switching your gender to the opposite sex. You wake up in the morning and are the opposite gender. All memories of your previous gender are erased. What is the first thing that you do as a man or a woman? . . . How do you feel about yourself when you look into the mirror? . . . How do you feel about your body? . . . Which part do you like? Which part is your least favorite?

What are you thinking when getting dressed? What image do you want to portray? . . . What will you have for breakfast?

How do you prepare yourself to go to work? . . . How do people treat you when you arrive? . . . How do your colleagues behave towards you? Do female and male colleagues treat you differently? . . . How do you sit? How do you walk? . . . Are you comfortable? . . . Are there equal numbers of men and women around you at work or do you feel marginal? . . . Do you feel you have more privileges or less than the opposite gender?

What happens when you want to share your opinions at the staff meeting? How do people react to your speaking up? Do they listen more or less to you than to others? Are you interrupted? . . . What do people expect from you? . . . What role do you usually play in small groups?

Do you try to please people or do you feel entitled to have your way? . . . Do you need help to do things or you feel capable of doing whatever you want? . . . What are you most careful about when talking to your boss? . . . Which gender is your boss? . . . Are you concerned about sexual harassment? . . . Do you feel that you can have an equal access to promotions?

What kind of conversations do you have during your lunch break? . . . What are you eating? What do you have in mind when choosing your food? . . . Are you lunching with a group or only one person? . . . Do you talk about food, relationships, sports, weekend activities, or personal struggles? . . . Who are you telling these things to: men or women? Do you say different things to men and women? Do they listen differently?

*What do people think of you? Do they see you as strong, inde-
pendent, and responsible or as insecure, needing reassurance
and advice? . . . What would you like people to think of
you? . . . Are you satisfied with your relationships and how
people treat you?*

*What kind of activities do you most enjoy with a close friend or a
colleague? . . . What makes you feel good about yourself? . . .
What makes you feel bad about yourself?*

*You finish working late in the evening; what do you think about
while walking to your car? Do you feel safe or are you on guard?
Do you feel confident about your ability to deal with whatever
could happen? . . . How do men look at you on the street? How
do women look at you on the street? . . . What do you think
about while driving? . . . What will be the first thing that you
will do when you get home tonight?*

What is your goal in life? . . . Who or what is your priority?

*When talking on the phone to your mother, what advice does she
have for you as a man or a woman? . . . What advice does your
father have for you as a man or a woman? . . . Would they give
you a different advice if you were the opposite gender?*

*What do you most like about your gender? . . . When you
watch TV, in which roles do you see member of your
gender? . . . What are your dreams for yourself in five years
from now? . . . In ten years from now? . . . What will you be
most proud of when you are older? . . . What will people
remember you for when you are gone?*

3. Conclude the exercise using some of the following questions for
   discussion:

   - What did you discover in this exercise?

   - Were you surprised at how your life could change?

   - Did you like the switch of gender? If you could choose your
     gender, which one would you prefer?

- How did it feel to be the opposite gender?
- How were you affected most by such a change?
- What was different in your life?
- Did people treat you the same way?
- Who was most likely to treat you differently?
- Were there things that you could then do that you can't do now or vice versa, things that you enjoy doing now that became restricted?
- Did your responsibilities change?
- How did people look at you?
- What privileges were different?
- How will this exercise affect your relationships with each gender?

4. Pass out the **Gender Differences and Stereotypes** worksheet and discuss which items participants can relate to.

GENDER DIFFERENCES AND STEREOTYPES

	WOMEN	MEN
1. Identity and sense of worth	defined by relationships	defined by success and work
2. Focus in conversations	extra attentive to others' needs and reactions	attentive to facts and hierarchy
3. Decision process	more feeling oriented	more thought oriented
4. Goal of communication	connectedness	exchange of information and negotiation of status
5. Interprets problem-talk as	an experience of closeness	a request for advice
6. Needs when having a problem	to be listened, understood and supported	to be alone or share the facts and find a solution
7. Social constraints/expectations	to look good, please and be in a relationship	to be strong, invulnerable and independent
8. Cost of gender role	health endangered, lack of power, lack of voice	isolation, unaware of own/other's needs, search meaning
9. Struggles	self-criticism, self-doubt, guilt, lack of entitlement	self-comparison, hide vulnerabilities, seek power/control
10. Fear	abandonment	engulfment
11. Worries about	being pushed away	being pushed around
12. Feels intimate	when talking and sharing personal information	when doing an activity
13. Same sex friendships	are actively sought and created	just happen or are created by the work environment
14. Uncomfortable with	anger	emotions in general, sadness in particular
15. Will more readily	give suggestions	give orders or information
16. Often assumes opinions	are just hypothesis and may be wrong	are real facts and are therefore right
17. When questioned	will more readily doubt oneself	will more readily defend or attack
18. Commitment	is a desirable goal	is a frightening idea
19. Jealous of	emotional closeness	sexual interaction
20. Feels responsible for	the quality of the relationship	the financial security and material comfort
21. Experience of anger is	mostly destructive to self (depression, self-hate)	mostly destructive towards others (violence)
22. Comfortable	with multi-tasking	with fewer tasks at a time
23. Prefers to work	collaboratively	competitively
24. Asking for help means	asking for cooperation	admitting to be lesser than the other person
25. When faced with a conflict	will more likely question and blame oneself	will more likely question and blame others
26. Language	includes deeper meanings, feelings and ideas	has literal signification

Cultures and Meanings

This game invites people to notice the experience of visiting or living in another culture. A context is created in which participants inadvertently make social errors with behaviors that would be acceptable in their usual culture. Participants develop an understanding of how groups of people are different and how meaning is constructed socially.

Goals

To notice how meanings are ascribed by contexts and cultures.

To become aware of how we deal with unknown differences.

To get an experiential glimpse at the experience of discrimination.

Group size

Unlimited.

Time

30–45 minutes.

Materials

None.

Process

1. Share the goals of the exercise with participants, then form two equal size groups based on who would like to host a party and who would prefer to be a guest, and provide the following information:

   ■ Much of what we perceive to be the truth and what we believe to be right or wrong is in reality "socially constructed." In other words, the culture in which you live trains you to believe that certain ideas are better than others, that certain ways of being are normal and others are not.

- The culture in which you live provides filters, frames of reference and norms that often are followed without questioning. For example, in the American culture it is generally expected that men will rarely or never cry, that women must be thin to be beautiful, that you should serve a meal to your guests first, and that grieving the death of a loved one requires expressions of sadness.

- It is important to become aware that many other perspectives are possible. For example, in some Arabic and South American cultures a skinny woman is considered very ugly while an overweight woman is considered wise and strong. In Italy, guests are often served last as the best part of several pasta dishes are at the bottom of the casserole. In Papua New Guinea, members of some tribes grieve the death of loved ones by making a joyful celebration around their burning bodies and then sharing a beverage containing the ashes so the dead person can live in all of them and provide them with extra strength, courage, and skills.

- In other words, the meaning ascribed to feelings and behaviors is determined by your culture.

- In order to notice some of our social constructions, this exercise will simulate the experience of arriving in a very different culture.

2. Assign a culture and a maximum of two or three vocabulary code words to each group. Make sure that the groups hear only their own code words.

☞ *The code words are listed and defined on page 165. Feel free to add your own words to the list.*

3. Once a group has learned their cultural vocabulary code words, invite both groups to socialize at an embassy cocktail party:

- At this party, it's important to be sensitive to cultural differences and avoid social errors.

- If a person you are speaking to violates your cultural norms, be sure to react with disapproval.

- The goal of this game is to guess each other's code words so you can stop offending people.

☞ *With beginning or more reserved groups it may be helpful to have them practice socializing in their own subgroups for a few minutes before inviting the other group to join in. You may also chose to have only one group assigned to differing social norms.*

4. After participants have socialized for approximately 10–20 minutes depending on the size of the group, ask them to reconvene in a circle to discuss their experience. The following questions may be asked:

   - What did you notice yourself thinking and feeling in that context?

   - How was the experience of being disapproved of when you said something that was completely normal for you?

   - Did you take it personally and feel inadequate?

     (That is very often the experience that international students have. Women, in general, question what they have done wrong when they receive an unanticipated response to their statements or actions.)

   - Had anyone experienced these feelings when in another culture or when spending some time with your partner's family if they are very different from you?

     (Behaviors that often have different connotations and meanings in families public expressions of affection).

   - How was it to have a common word suddenly have negative connotations.

   - Did anyone noticed how the meaning we ascribe to words and things is completely arbitrary and socially determined?

   - How will the idea that most perceptions are not "truths" but socially constructed beliefs, norms and standards that are taught to you from infancy affect you now?

5. Conclude with the following statements:

- As adults you have the power and the right to revise your socially constructed beliefs and make your own choices regarding whether they make any sense for you.

- It is important to acknowledge that since they are not truths, some people may have completely different norms and perspectives that may be equally valid.

- People always have reasons behind what they do, feel, or say. It is important to be sensitive, aware, and respectful of cultural or social differences.

NEPTUNA VOCABULARY CODE WORDS

In Neptuna . . .

"Hi" is the abbreviation of "Hey Idiot."

"How are you" means "you really look awful."

"What do you like to do" means "I'm completely in love with you."

"Fun" is considered an extremely funny word.

"Yes" means no.

_____

_____

_____

ELIPTA VOCABULARY CODE WORDS

In Elipta . . .

"Sorry is considered an extremely funny word.

"No" means yes.

"Thank you" means "I hated it."

Looking in the eyes while talking means I want to spend the night with you.

"See" means you are extremely beautiful.

_____

_____

_____

Discovering Each Other's Values

Participants are invited to notice how their image or story of their intimate partner fits with the reality of who that person really is.

Goals

To identify and prioritize your own values.

To identify and prioritize what you think are your partner's values.

To accept and appreciate your differences.

Group size

Unlimited number of couples.

Time

30–45 minutes.

Materials

Values worksheet; pencils.

☞ *This exercise is best done when a level of acceptance of each other's differences have already been reached. Done too early, participants may have difficulty accepting differences and the exercise may cause distress and conflicts.*

Process

1. Introduce the goals; distribute the **Values** worksheets and pencils; then provide the following instructions:

   ■ In the left column on your worksheet, list the values you hold in order of their importance to you.

   ■ In the right column, list in order of importance the values you believe your partner holds.

   ■ When you have both completed your lists, compare them and talk about them in a respectful way.

■ Partners, you may now find an area of the room away from other participants and begin your list.

2. When everyone is done, reconvene the group and conclude the activity by asking the participants to answer some of the following questions:

   ■ Was it hard to guess your partner's priorities in terms of values?

   ■ Was there a discrepancy between what you imagined your partner's hierarchy of values to be and what it really was?

   ■ How does it affect your relationship to know these things?

   ■ Does it make it easier to understand each other and accept these differences now that they are more visible?

VALUES

Your values	Your partner's values

Hand Exercise

In this exercise, participants are invited to be mindful about the experience of physical contact. Through the exploration of a hand, individuals learn to be present and aware of the different aspects of touch. A good exercise to conclude a workshop series.

Goals

To practice being present and mindful.

To be fully connected with one's body and experiences.

To pay attention to one's preferred experiences around touch.

To experiment with different ways of touching.

Group size

2–20 participants.

Time

30–40 minutes.

Materials

Tibetan or meditation bell.

Process

1. Introduce the exercise by presenting some of the following information and offering your own examples:

   ■ Our mind has a natural tendency to wander, into the past and into the future. Even when we are involved in a pleasant experience such as watching a beautiful sunset, getting a massage, or exchanging caresses with an intimate partner, we are often not fully present. Thinking about work or worrying about the consequences of an action often carry our mind away.

- In a relationship it is important to be able to fully appreciate being with a partner. Often, with everyone's busy schedule, little time is left for those pleasurable moments, so it is worth the effort of experiencing them fully.

- In this exercise, you will be invited to focus on all the details of your experience and practice being mindful by exploring the touching of the hand of another participant (or of your intimate partner).

2. Give the following instructions:

   - If any of you would prefer to do this exercise alone, feel free to simply take a chair and find a comfortable place in the room by yourself, then relax while those who prefer to have a partner form teams.

   - Those of you who feel comfortable having a partner, walk slowly and randomly in the room until you come across someone you feel comfortable with. You will know that person also feels comfortable working with you if he or she slows down or stops in front of you at the same time you stop. If someone doesn't stop even though you are stopping, it doesn't necessarily mean anything about you as a person but only that she or he doesn't know you as well as other participants, doesn't feel comfortable participating in this exercise with members of your gender, or possibly feels too eager to engage in the exercise with you and thus chooses to avoid taking a risk.

   - When you select a partner, take two chairs and find a place in the room to sit face to face with about one foot between your two chairs.

   - Decide who will be the leader and who will be the receiver. You will be switching roles in 10 minutes.

   - Sit comfortably on a chair, uncross your legs, breath deeply, and relax. Receivers who feel comfortable doing so may close their eyes to be fully connected with their experience.

■ Receivers, extend one hand, open and palm down, so that the leader can gently hold it comfortably in one hand and explore with the other.

3. Read the following mindfulness meditation script, slowly and softly, allowing time to focus on the experience. Pause for 15 seconds after each paragraph.

Leaders, start by very slowly sliding your hand on the top of your partner's hand a few times as you focus on the sensations. The secret of this exercise is for you to go very slowly and for both of you to be fully present to all the dimensions of touching.

You may notice at times that your mind wanders somewhere else. Gently bring it back to the exercise. It is part of the nature of the mind to wander around. As the Buddist writer Jack Kornfield puts it, the mind is like a puppy, you tell it to stay, and it will stay for a few minutes but wander around again until you bring it back and tell it to stay again.

Now bring your focus to the movement, noticing how each millimeter of your hand feels like when touched or when touching. Is the temperature of the skin warm or cold, is it the same for every part of the hand, is it different at the level of joints or the nails? How does the temperature of your hand contrast with your partner's?

Gently change from using your entire hand to simply using a finger or two. Do you get the same sensations when the thumb is exploring as when each of the fingers is exploring? How about when the tip of a nail is gently exploring? How does it feel like to touch a bone or the muscles? Can you feel the pulse when you touch the veins in the hand?

How would you describe to an alien what it is like to touch a human hand? Are there any hairs? Any irregularities in the skin? How about the skin between the fingers? Is it softer or different in any way to the skin on the top of the hand or at the joints? How about the side of the fingers? When you are touching the side of a finger can you still tell the difference between touching a muscle and a joint? What do you notice? What does it feel like to touch a nail, the tip of the nail, the merging of the nail in the skin?

Continue breathing deeply and focusing on your experiences of touch. You may notice at times that your mind wanders somewhere else. Gently bring it back to the exercise. It is part of the nature of the mind to wander.

Now turn the receiver's hand so that its palm is facing the ceiling. How different is the inside of the hand? Are there more creases? Is it softer? Can you actually feel the lines in the hand? Take a few minutes to explore all the details of the palm and the fingers, millimeter by millimeter?

Do you feel the blood flowing in any part of the hand? Do you feel your own pulse or your partner's? Is it moist or completely dry? How would you describe the texture?

If you let your hand rest still in your partner's hand, what do you notice? Are your hands vibrating or are they completely still? What happens if you float a couple of millimeters above it, do you still feel some heat? How far above the hand can you float and still feel some energy?

Come back to resting your hand in your partner's hand. How does the stillness feel.

Breathe in deeply, imagining the air going through your nose, down your throat, into your arm, and down in each finger. What does it feel like? Imagine the air moving in your body as if a wave was coming and going. How does it feel like to have air at the tip of your fingers? How does the contact feel now? Take a few minutes to experience that.

When you are ready to withdraw your hand, gently press the hand of your partner and wait until you have a response, until your partner presses back, then mutually withdraw your hands. Take a deep breath and switch roles.

4. Reread the script while the other partner leads. At the end of the second time, tell participants to take a deep breath, ring a Tibetan meditation bell and tell participants to open their eyes when they don't hear the vibrations of the bell anymore.

5. Conclude the activity by inviting participants to discuss their experience and how being present and mindful could be helpful in a relationship.

References and Inspirations

The following books provided inspiration for games, ideas, philosophy, and theory.

Improvisation and creativity

Campbell, Andrea. *Great Games for Great Parties*. New York, NY: Sterling Publishing Company, Inc., 1991.

Fluegelman, Andrew, editor. *The New Games Book*. Garden City, NY: Doubleday & Co., 1976.

Fluegelman, Andrew, editor. *More New Games,*. Garden City, NY: Doubleday & Co., 1976.

Hoper, Claus, Ulrike Kutzleb, Alke Stobbe, and Bertram Weber. *Awareness Games: Personal Growth through Group Interaction*. New York, NY: St. Martin's Press, 1974.

Spolin, Viola. *Improvisation for the Theater*. Evanston, IL: Northwestern University Press, 1963.

Weinstein, Matt, and Joel Goodman. *Playfair*. San Luis Obispo, CA: Impact Publishers, 1980.

Narrative therapy

Freedman, J., and G. Combs. *Narrative Therapy: The Social Construction of Preferred Realities*. New York, NY: Norton Company Inc., 1996.

Friedman, S. *The Reflecting Team in Action: Collaborative Practice in Family Therapy*. New York, NY: Guilford Press, 1995.

Monk, G., J. Winslade, K. Crocket, and D. Epston. *Narrative therapy in practice: The Archeology of Hope*. San Francisco, CA: Jossey-Bass Publishers, 1997.

White, M. *Re-authoring lives: Interviews & Essays*. Adelaide, Australia: Dulwich Centre Publications, 1995.

White, M., and D. Epston. *Narrative Means to Therapeutic Ends.* New York, NY: Norton Company Inc., 1990.

Zimmerman, J., and V. Dickerson. (1994). Using a narrative metaphor: Implications for theory and clinical practice. *Family Process*, 33, 233–245.

Zimmerman, J., and V. Dickerson. *If problems talked: Narrative therapy in action.* New York, NY: Guilford Press, 1996.

Note

Since so much of our knowledge and ideas come from reading, sharing, and talking with others, we have found it difficult to make a complete and thorough list of all the sources of our inspiration. We have done our best to acknowledge all the individuals and manuscripts whose work influenced us. Despite our best efforts, however, we are aware that we may have inadvertently omitted some references and would like to apologize in advance for the unintended omission.

WORKING WITH GROUPS ON FAMILY ISSUES

Sandy Stewart Christian, MSW, LICSW, Editor

These 24 structured exercises combine the knowledge of marriage and family experts with practical techniques to help you move individuals, couples, and families toward positive change. Topics include divorce, single parenting, stepfamilies, gay and lesbian relationships, working partners, and more.

❑ **Working with Groups on Family Issues / $24.95**
❑ **Worksheet Masters / $9.95**

HEALING FOR ADULT SURVIVORS
OF CHILDHOOD SEXUAL ABUSE

Bonnie Collins, EdM, CSW-R, and Kathryn Marsh, CSW-R

As many as 20 percent of girls are sexually abused. In this manual, you will find a complete 12-session program for treating clients whose problems stem from the sexual abuse they experienced as children.

❑ **Healing for Adult Survivors of Childhood Sexual Abuse / $24.95**
❑ **Worksheet Masters / $9.95**

WORKING WITH GROUPS IN THE WORKPLACE

BRIDGING THE GENDER GAP

Louise Yolton Eberhardt

Bridging the Gender Gap contains a wealth of exercises for trainers to use in gender role awareness groups, diversity training, couples workshops, college classes, and youth seminars.

❑ **Bridging the Gender Gap / $24.95**
❑ **Worksheet Masters / $9.95**

CONFRONTING SEXUAL HARASSMENT

Louise Yolton Eberhardt

Confronting Sexual Harassment presents exercises that trainers can safely use with groups to constructively explore the issues of sexual harassment, look at the underlying causes, understand the law, motivate men to become allies, and empower women to speak up.

❑ **Confronting Sexual Harassment / $24.95**
❑ **Worksheet Masters / $9.95**

CELEBRATING DIVERSITY

Cheryl Hetherington

Celebrating Diversity helps people confront and question the beliefs, prejudices, and fears that can separate them from others. Carefully written exercises help trainers present these sensitive issues in the workplace as well as in educational settings.

❑ **Celebrating Diversity / $24.95**
❑ **Worksheet Masters / $9.95**

Call 1-800-247-6789 to receive a catalog or to place an order for any Whole Person Associates product.

ADDITIONAL TRAINERS RESOURCES

MIND-BODY MAGIC

Martha Belknap, MA

Make any presentation more powerful with one of these 40 feel-good activities. Handy tips with each activity show you how to use it in your presentation, plus ideas for enhancing or extending the activity, and suggestions for adapting it for your teaching goals and audience. Use *Mind-Body Magic* to present any topic with pizzazz!

❑ **Mind-Body Magic / $21.95**
❑ **Worksheet Masters / $9.95**

INSTANT ICEBREAKERS
50 Powerful Catalysts for Group Interaction and High-Impact Learning

Sandy Stewart Christian, MSW, and
Nancy Loving Tubesing, EdD, Editors

Introduce the subject at hand and introduce participants to each other with these proven strategies that apply to all kinds of audiences and appeal to many learning styles. Step-by-step instructions make any presentation a breeze.

❑ **Instant Icebreakers / $24.95**
❑ **Worksheet Masters / $9.95**

PLAYING ALONG
37 Group Learning Activities Borrowed from Improvisational Theater

Izzy Gesell, MS

Set the stage for learning and growth with these innovative, playful activities borrowed from a classic art form: improvisational theater. Whatever your topic, these brief (5-10 minute) exercises activate the all-important learning skills of listening, accepting, affirming, imagining, and trusting—and pave the way for personal growth or organizational change.

❑ **Playing Along / $21.95**

CREATING A CLIMATE FOR POWER LEARNING
37 Mind-Stretching Activities

Carolyn Chambers Clark, EdD, ARNP

Creative warm-up processes that prepare leaders and participants for a satisfying learning experience. These activities will enhance your presentation skills, leadership style, and teaching effectiveness no matter what your audience or setting.

❑ **Creating a Climate for Power Learning / $21.95**

PLAYFUL ACTIVITIES FOR POWERFUL PRESENTATIONS

Bruce Williamson

Spice up presentations with healthy laughter. The 40 creative energizers in this book will enhance learning, stimulate communication, promote teamwork, and reduce resistance to group interaction.

❑ **Playful Activities for Powerful Presentations / $24.95**

MORE GROUP PROCESS RESOURCES

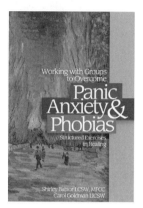

WORKING WITH GROUPS TO OVERCOME PANIC, ANXIETY, & PHOBIAS

Shirley Babior, LCSW, MFCC, and
Carol Goldman, LICSW

Written especially for therapists and group leaders, this manual presents well-researched, state-of-the-art treatment strategies and action-oriented client activities for a variety of anxiety disorders including:

● panic disorder
● generalized anxiety
● agoraphobia, social anxiety
● specific phobias, such as fear of flying

Sample treatment plans with behavioral goals and objectives make this book a priceless resource for therapists who must develop and document appropriate treatment protocols and strategies for clients served by managed-care organizations. Adapt your presentation for individual or group therapy or for worksite lectures and all-day workshops—the book's format makes it easy. Support groups also will find this manual helpful.

❏ **Working with Groups to Overcome Panic, Anxiety, & Phobias / $24.95**
❏ **Worksheet Masters / $9.95**

About the authors
Shirley Babior, a psychotherapist in private practice in San Diego, California, is codirector of the Center for Anxiety and Stress Treatment. Carol Goldman, a founding director of the Boston Institute of Cognitive-Behavior Therapies, is a therapist in private practice in Boston, Massachusetts.

OVERCOMING PANIC, ANXIETY, & PHOBIAS
Strategies to Free Yourself from Worry and Fear

Shirley Babior, LCSW, MFCC, and
Carol Goldman, LICSW

This practical handbook, recommended by experts in the field of anxiety disorders for people whose lives are upset by worry, fear, or panic, offers coping strategies based on the latest clinical research. Personal stories of recovery, worksheets for recording symptoms and progress, and information on finding professional help make this book a must-read for anxiety sufferers who want to regain control of their life.

❏ **Overcoming Panic, Anxiety, & Phobias / $12.95**

Call 1-800-247-6789 to receive a catalog or to place an order for any Whole Person Associates product.

A 10-WEEK RECOVERY PROGRAM FOR OVERCOMING PANIC, ANXIETY, & PHOBIAS

Shirley Babior, LCSW, MFCC, and Carol Goldman, LICSW

State-of-the-art cognitive-behavioral strategies endorsed by leading clinical experts provide panic relief and help listeners learn the skills they need to manage anxiety disorders before the problem gets out of control. This six-tape program also is ideal for helping clients reduce chronic stress and tension. The program includes:

- six audiotapes (ten instructional sessions plus the *Calm Down* tape, which features four relaxation scripts)
- worksheets with homework assignments to support each session
- *Overcoming Panic, Anxiety, & Phobias*, a practical self-help handbook of coping strategies

❑ **A 10-Week Recovery Program (six audiotapes, book, worksheets) / $95.00**

Therapists: Call for quantity discounts on 10-Week Panic Recovery Programs for your clients.

WORRY STOPPERS
Breathing & Imagery to Calm the Restless Mind
audiotape

These six calming visualization exercises will help you learn new ways to breathe, relax, clear your mind, and release tension.

❑ **Worry Stoppers / $11.95**

CALM DOWN
Relaxation & Imagery Skills for Managing Fear, Anxiety, Panic
audiotape

Turn off the panic button, breathe away stress, and experience total body relaxation.

❑ **Calm Down / $11.95**

Call 1-800-247-6789 to receive a catalog or to place an order for any Whole Person Associates product.

ADDITIONAL GROUP PROCESS RESOURCES

WORKING WITH WOMEN'S GROUPS
VOLUMES 1 & 2

Louise Yolton Eberhardt

When leading a women's group, don't just rely on personal experience and intuition—equip yourself with these volumes of proven exercises. Louise Yolton Eberhardt has distilled more than a quarter century of experience into nearly a hundred processes addressing the issues that are most important to women today.

The two volumes of *Working with Women's Groups* have been completely revised and updated. *Volume 1* explores consciousness raising, self-discovery, and assertiveness training. *Volume 2* looks at sexuality issues, women of color, and leadership skills training.

- ❏ **Working with Women's Groups, Vol. 1 / $24.95**
- ❏ **Working with Women's Groups, Vol. 2 / $24.95**
- ❏ **Worksheet Masters, Vol. 1 / $9.95**
- ❏ **Worksheet Masters, Vol. 2 / $9.95**

WORKING WITH MEN'S GROUPS

Roger Karsk and Bill Thomas

Working with Men's Groups has been updated to reflect the reality of men's lives in the 1990s. Each exercise follows a structured pattern to help trainers develop either onetime workshops or ongoing groups that explore men's issues in four key areas: self-discovery, consciousness raising, intimacy, and parenting.

- ❏ **Working with Men's Groups / $24.95**
- ❏ **Worksheet Masters / $9.95**

WORKING WITH GROUPS TO EXPLORE
FOOD & BODY CONNECTIONS

Sandy Stewart Christian, MSW, Editor

This collection of 36 group processes gathered from experts around the country tackles complex and painful issues nearly everyone is concerned about—dieting, weight, healthy eating, fitness, body image, and self-esteem—using a whole person approach that advocates health and fitness for people of all sizes.

- ❏ **Working with Groups to Explore**
   Food & Body Connections / $24.95
- ❏ **Worksheet Masters / $9.95**

Call 1-800-247-6789 to receive a catalog or to place an order for any Whole Person Associates product.